MENTORING

PRINCIPALS

In tribute to
Norman and Frances Kendrick
and
Roy and Carol Sheets
and
Howard and Winifred Young
who were our first and most influential mentors;
our wives
Gina Knight
and
Kerry Sheets
and
Gertrude Young

who support us with their unending love and encouragement;
and the many other principal mentor-mentee partnerships
that we hope will be able to develop into as meaningful
and fulfilling a relationship as ours.

MENTORING

PRINCIPALS

Frameworks, Agendas, Tips, and Case Stories for Mentors and Mentees

PAUL G. YOUNG
JEROMEY M. SHEETS
DUSTIN D. KNIGHT

A Joint Publication

CORWIN PRESS
A SAGE Publications Company
Thousand Oaks, California

NATIONAL ASSOCIATION OF ELEMENTARY SCHOOL PRINCIPALS
Serving All Elementary and Middle Level Principals

For information:

Corwin Press, Inc.
A Sage Publications Company
2455 Teller Road
Thousand Oaks, California 91320
www.corwinpress.com

Sage Publications Ltd.
1 Oliver's Yard
55 City Road
London EC1Y 1SP
United Kingdom

Sage Publications India Pvt. Ltd.
B-42, Panchsheel Enclave
Post Box 4109
New Delhi 110 017 India

Printed in the United States of America.

Library of Congress Cataloging-in-Publication Data

Young, Paul G., 1950–
    Mentoring principals: frameworks, agendas, tips, and case stories for mentors and mentees / by Paul G. Young, Jeromey M. Sheets, Dustin D. Knight.
        p. cm.
    Includes bibliographical references and index.
    ISBN 1-4129-0515-X (cloth) — ISBN 1-4129-0516-8 (pbk.)
        1. School principals—In-service training—Case studies. 2. Mentoring in education—Case studies. I. Sheets, Jeromey M. II. Knight, Dustin D. III. Title.
    LB2831.9.Y68 2005
    371.2′012—dc22

                                            2004026605

This book is printed on acid-free paper.

05   06   07   08   09   10   9   8   7   6   5   4   3   2   1

Acquisitions Editor:	Jean Ward
Production Editor:	Kristen Gibson
Copy Editor:	Diana Breti
Typesetter:	C&M Digitals (P) Ltd.
Indexer:	Jean Casalegno
Proofreader:	Carole Quandt
Cover Designer:	Michael Dubowe

Contents

Foreword

The Mentor: taken from Greek mythology, loyal friend of Odysseus, left in charge of Odysseus's household and son. By definition, a "wise and trusted counselor."

My definition would be simpler: a professional person who recognizes the need to promote his or her profession—the professional who not only will give back to his or her profession, but by doing so, really invests in the future of the profession by paying forward.

The three authors of this book know the meaning of mentor and mentee. Each has given and received knowledge, strength, and love that will make each a better person and a better professional through his experiences. The mentees can look back on the experience and now begin modeling for others what they have learned. The mentor has "planted his field" and with a little water and fertilizer can watch it grow into a productive crop, which can be passed on for growth. The chain should never be broken.

This book, *Mentoring Principals,* contains six distinctive sections:

First, supporting data and rationale for mentoring;

Second, a guide to begin your own mentor program, whether with one person or several;

Third, a set of formal mentoring agendas spanning the academic year and linked to NAESP standards for principals;

Fourth, stories of job-embedded mentoring-in-the-moment as told frankly by the mentor; enriched by the reflections of his two mentees; recording both sides of their triumphs, their frustrations, their challenges; providing an authentic case study of how, in this partnership, each worked to make the other successful and together they turned crises and crunch times into professional growth opportunities. Readers are very likely to relate these stories to the everyday experiences of their own learning and professional development;

Fifth, widening the lens from this case study to exemplary mentoring practice around the country, lead mentors share words of wisdom, tips for mentors, their own stories, and lessons learned;

Last, the authors reflect on how the mentoring partnership has impacted and been of value to their professional development and job performance.

Reading the stories and reflections in Part IV, sometimes you will laugh, sometimes you will say "that happened to me," and sometimes you will just scratch your head.

You too can create an experience for yourself and some other professional by reading this book and following some of the suggestions, noting some of the pitfalls, but more importantly, giving your knowledge and skill learned from the smooth pavement or rough road you have traveled in your professional life.

While this book centers on school administrators, it can be applied to any job, profession, or station in life. A "wise and trusted counselor" is a valuable asset for anyone.

D. Richard Murray
Executive Director Emeritus
Ohio Association of Elementary School Administrators

Preface

There are books and resource materials for mentoring in the business section of bookstores, but few exist that specifically describe for elementary and middle-level principals what mentoring is, how it's done, or what outcomes are possible. By writing this book, we hope to contribute authentic information that in a variety of ways might fulfill that need. The literature for the business world is designed to help people become better leaders and advance in their careers. This book is designed to help elementary and middle-level principals gain insights that will enable them to do the same.

We envision this book being of primary value—but not limited to—the following audiences:

- Students and faculty engaged in college or university administrative training programs
- Aspiring principals
- Practicing principals
- Assistant principals
- Retired principals
- Association leaders
- Boards of education
- Superintendents, assistant superintendents
- Directors, supervisors, educational support personnel
- Service industry personnel
- Teachers
- Interested constituencies

As the legions of baby boomer principals retire, trained, effective mentors are critically needed to help "pass the torch" of leadership in our nation's schools. Mentors know how to impart lessons in the "art" of being a principal. They share the "ins and outs" of the job that are unlikely to be learned from any other professional. They see their protégés and mentees in ways they have never considered themselves before, helping them develop into leaders in a world of change.

This book contains an overview of the key components and phases of principal mentoring and adult learning. It provides the architecture for formal mentoring. For aspiring mentors and mentees, a set of meeting agendas linked to NAESP standards for principals are included. It also features authentic stories, reflections, and lessons learned from a mentor and his protégés. Additionally, the book draws on the mentoring experiences and wisdom of expert mentors around the country. It is intended to support the need for a trained cadre of certified mentors, provide direction in the "art" and "how to" of mentoring, and to share learning and practice with others.

Effective principal mentoring must be grounded in learning. We have attempted to share what we've learned as well as how we did it. Writing about our experiences has required hours of reflection. It was very beneficial. Together, we've learned much about ourselves and grown. As a result, we are better prepared to meet daily challenges, share our joys and sorrows with others, and model the art of being an effective principal.

> *Principals must teach their 'craft' and support the 'superstars' who will make outstanding principals.*
>
> *Every effective, practicing principal should identify, encourage, and nurture at least five aspiring principals before he or she retires or leaves the principalship.*
>
> *Everything in an effective mentoring program for principals must be focused on ensuring learning for both the mentee and the mentor and ultimately the students.*

—Paul G. Young, 2003

Acknowledgments

This book could not have been written without the encouragement, assistance, and support of many individuals dear to us all. First, we extend our gratitude to superintendents Lawrence Burgess and Thomas Maher, the members of the Lancaster Board of Education, and colleagues in the Lancaster (Ohio) City Schools, who have enabled our leadership abilities to emerge and grow. They have encouraged and acknowledged our work, and allowed us to share with others in countless ways.

Second, we thank the board of directors of the National Association of Elementary School Principals (NAESP) and the visionary leadership team of Vince Ferrandino, Gail Gross, and Deborah Reeve for their recognition of our mentoring model and encouragement to share what we know and do in this book. We also thank numerous colleagues in Ohio and across the nation who have shared ideas and best practices that have influenced our partnership.

We thank Jean Ward, Senior Acquisitions Editor, and all the staff at Corwin Press for their acknowledgment and support of our work. We are indebted for their service that has enabled us to share our case studies with a vast audience.

Last, we thank our wives and families for their understanding, patience, love, and inspiration. Their unselfish sacrifices have given us time to talk, share, engage in a variety of mentoring activities, write, and produce our stories to share with others.

Paul G. Young, Jeromey M. Sheets,
and Dustin D. Knight
Lancaster, Ohio

Corwin Press would like to thank the following reviewers for their contributions to this book.

Lynn Babcock, EdD
Past President, NAESP
Past Chair and Member, PALS Advisory Team, NAESP
Dexter, MI

Marci Brueggen
Retired Principal
Oklahoma City, OK

Sandra Harris, PhD
Director, Center for Research and Doctoral Studies
   in Educational Leadership
Lamar University
Beaumont, TX

Rosemarie Young, EdD
President, NAESP
Principal
Louisville, KY

About the Authors

 **Paul G. Young** is the principal of West Elementary School in Lancaster, Ohio. He began his career 30 years ago as a high school band director, then after 11 years retrained as an elementary school teacher and principal. He taught fourth grade before accepting his first principalship in 1986.

He served as president of the Ohio Association of Elementary School Administrators in 1997. He was elected to the NAESP board of directors in 1998, was elected president-elect in 2001, and served as president in 2002–2003.

He strongly believes in the importance of the arts in a well-balanced school curriculum. He also stresses the importance of aspiring principals' programs and the development of mentoring programs (such as NAESP's PALS Corps) for the next generation of principals. He strives to focus national attention on the restructuring of the principalship, rekindling respect for the principalship and public education, and balance and alternatives to the high-stakes testing currently engulfing schools across the nation.

Dr. Young completed his degrees at Ohio University, Athens, Ohio. He is an adjunct professor of music at Ohio University-Lancaster. His wife, Gertrude, is an elementary vocal and instrumental music teacher with Lancaster City Schools. They are proud parents of two daughters. Katie, a graduate of the Eastman School of Music, University of Rochester, and Rice University in Houston, Texas, is an oboist with the New World Symphony in Miami. Mary Ellen is a senior business and marketing major at the University of Cincinnati.

He is the author of *You Have to Go to School, You're the Principal: 101 Tips to Make It Better for Your Students, Your Staff and Yourself* (Corwin Press) and co-author of *Mastering the Art of Mentoring Principals* (with protégé Jeromey Sheets), available through NAESP and KGE Press, Arlington, Va.

Jeromey M. Sheets was born and raised in Nelsonville, a small town in southeastern Ohio. His success as a student-athlete helped him to obtain admission to Heidelberg College in Tiffin, Ohio, where he earned a baccalaureate degree in elementary education and enjoyed success as an intercollegiate wrestler.

After graduation, he taught a combined second/third grade in Lancaster where he began working for Paul Young. After one year of teaching, he enrolled at Ashland University and completed the coursework for principal's certification and earned a master's degree within two years. In mid-March, 2002, he became the principal of North Elementary School in Lancaster.

He is the Zone I representative for the board of directors of the Ohio Association of Elementary School Administrators. He has presented at OAESA and NAESP professional conferences and conventions. He is the co-author of the book *Mastering the Art of Mentoring Principals* with his mentor, Paul Young.

He and his wife Kerry live in Lancaster.

Dustin D. Knight grew up in the suburbs of Columbus, Ohio. He earned a baccalaureate degree in elementary education at Ohio University. He began teaching in a small rural school district as a full-time substitute. He was a middle school language arts teacher prior to teaching third grade at West Elementary School.

He completed his master's degree in educational administration at Ashland University. He became principal of Bloom Elementary School, Lithopolis, Ohio, in late August, 2002. He returned to Lancaster and worked as the interim principal of West Elementary School for the 2002–2003 school year. He is now the principal of Chief Tarhe Elementary School in Lancaster. He has been a regular presenter at both the OAESA Aspiring Principals Conference and Annual Professional Conference and Trade Show.

He and his wife, Gina, enjoy family time with their young children, son Spencer and daughter Chloe. They live in Lancaster with their golden retriever, Mulligan.

If you want staff, students, and parents to respect you, you must first earn their trust.

—Dustin D. Knight

Character cannot be developed in ease and quiet. Only through experience of trial and suffering can the soul be strengthened, ambition inspired, and success achieved.

—Helen Keller

Coming together is a beginning. Staying together is a process. Working together is success.

—Henry Ford

A leader has been defined as one that knows the way, goes the way, and shows the way.

—Author Unknown

Introduction

The only people who really understand the breadth of the principal-ship are other principals. Despite the years of preparation, beginning principals really learn how to be a principal by practicing. And their learning is best guided, nurtured, and supported by another wise, experienced, and caring principal.

This book describes the important components of principal mentoring. It began with the real experiences of the three authors: mentor Paul Young and Dustin and Jeromey, his mentees. Consideration of the nature of mentoring and guidelines for practice are offered in Part I. Part II describes key mentoring responsibilities and ways to approach them. Part III presents sample agendas for focused mentor-mentee discussion and reflection in dedicated time set aside for "formal" mentoring meetings. These agendas follow NAESP standards and principles and are sequenced to anticipate the demands that the school calendar is likely to place on the new school principal. The authentic stories of Part IV detail the trials and tribulations of two beginning principals and their partnership with an experienced, passionate mentor and highlight the lessons learned, together with the mentoring interaction and the reflection of the partners. Expanding outward, additional mentoring wisdom and stories are shared in Part V by outstanding principals and mentors from around the country. Part VI offers the reflections and insights of the three authors from their perspectives in the mentoring relationship and partnership. They respond to a set of questions that the reader can use to reflect on his or her own experience as a principal, a mentor, or mentee, or to inform development of a new mentoring program or partnership. The authors close with their conclusions and shared wisdom for those undertaking the mentoring experience so needed for the development of outstanding principals.

By reading the stories, reflecting on the lessons to be learned, and sharing with others, prospective mentors and mentees can gain valuable insights into shaping their unique mentoring partnership. They can identify the pitfalls to avoid. From the experiences described in this book, they can learn the processes, activities, and phases of principal mentoring.

Principal mentoring must always be focused on learning: the mentee's learning, often the mentor's co-learning, and always, ultimately, student learning. On the pages that follow, enjoy what the authors and contributors offer to their leadership educational colleagues.

Part I

The Architecture
of Mentoring

MENTORING SCHOOL PRINCIPALS

Why is it that some principals quickly learn to do their jobs in an effective manner while others stumble? The curriculum in most college and university programs covers school business and finance, law, public relations, school politics, communication, collective bargaining, data collection and analysis, evaluations, community relations, current issues, curriculum and instruction, and broader leadership, so beginning principals have similar training and preparation. The programs prepare students to read, write, and think critically. They are rigorous. They are beneficial. They are a requirement for certification and licensure in most states. They are enjoyable times to reflect and learn with others.

But they are not end-all learning programs for principals. They are preservice programs that equip aspiring principals with just a small portion of the knowledge that is necessary to effectively master the realities of the principalship. Those principals who think their learning stops once they've completed the college or university program will most predictably fail. That has been, and continues to be, the historical outcome for far too many beginning principals. The real learning for the principal begins when he or she is handed the keys to the school. And those who eventually succeed can identify one or more influential people who were very effective in helping them learn the important things about being principal. Those key individuals are mentors.

Used as a noun, a mentor is a wise and trusted counselor or teacher. But as a verb, as in "to mentor a beginning principal," it is more about a partnership of learning—both for the mentor and the mentee. Learning is the most important part of an effective mentoring program, and it is ongoing. When learning is not the primary focus, the partnership fails. In programs designed for mentoring teachers, most often a seasoned veteran is paired with a novice. There are many formalized programs that prescribe various objectives to be accomplished in some observable manner. The objectives focus on pedagogy, classroom management, formal and informal rules of the school, and a variety of other lessons necessary for learning the tricks of the trade. When the prescribed learning outcomes are met, the relationship frequently recedes to a level of friendship because the goals of mentoring are achieved.

Principals need similar kinds of support, but much, much more. Becoming an effective principal takes time, even years. It is hard to group all of the on-the-job learning objectives into any prescribed curriculum. Continuous learning and growth require reflection and an interconnected relationship among two or more people with an understanding of adult learner needs. Despite this acknowledged awareness and understanding, there are far too few school districts where formal or even informal mentoring programs for principals exist. Most beginning principals are left to find a mentor in their own way.

Beginning principals face a quandary. Where does one find a mentor? What are the qualities of an effective mentor? Who is a "principal" mentor? What does it mean to be a mentee, or a protégé? Is there a difference? What are the roles and responsibilities? How do certain people make something that is elusive work and come together?

In much of the literature, mentee and protégé are words that have evolved to interchangeably describe the novice learner. Most people envision the mentor as someone who shares knowledge and influences their lives. Most everyone can think of one or more personal examples of such people. In this book, protégé refers to one who was identified, encouraged, and nurtured by an experienced colleague prior to becoming a principal. The protégé received unconditional and faithful acceptance from his or her mentor. The mentor recognized the protégé's ability and talent and committed himself or herself to helping develop that potential. A mentee is one who arrives at the threshold of the principalship without having been a protégé, yet is just as much in need as he or she begins learning the realities of the principalship. For the mentee, the partnership must be created; for the protégé, there was a more natural evolution over time.

For practical purposes, mentee and protégé are used interchangeably in this book. For any beginning principal, whether they've been groomed for the job as a protégé or not, the learning curve is steep. In one hand they have the keys to their new school, and in the other they need the hand of an effective mentor who will guide and nurture them toward mastery of the keys to becoming a successful, effective principal.

CREATING THE PARTNERSHIP

It is critical that practicing principals assume responsibility for creating meaningful and successful mentor-mentee partnerships. There is a tremendous need. But are all practicing principals capable or even willing? The answer is no.

Mentors love learning even more than teaching. They prefer to share rather that dominate, give rather than receive. By investing time in the partnership, they often learn as much or more than their mentee. In effective principal mentoring partnerships, wisdom is discovered through a learning relationship that enables both the mentor and the mentee to better understand the needs of the individual and the school. Mentors are less an authority figure, more a facilitator of learning. Rather than mentor driven, with the mentor assuming full responsibility for the mentee's learning, the principal mentoring partnership is based upon shared responsibilities, priorities, and principles of adult learning.

Qualities for Mentors

Practicing principals who become mentors must have a strong desire to learn and be willing to commit time toward that end. They must be capable of deep reflection and open to sharing their inner thoughts and feelings. They must admit their mistakes and teach and model by example. They must be able to identify and avoid the pitfalls of mentoring relationships. They must never think of mentoring as a chore. Those who strive to develop the most successful partnerships will realize a sense of pride and accomplishment that matters more than any amount of money.

Mentors must be capable of reflecting deeply upon their own experiences from a variety of vantage points, reaching deep levels of understanding, and sharing their learning with the mentee in meaningful, practical ways. They must clearly understand and recount their own professional career path and choices. They must be aware of the major events and life experiences that influenced them. Those who are skilled at critically reflecting on their own experiences will be best at modeling critical reflection for their mentee. They will help the mentee see and understand the connections. They must avoid trying to clone their mentee; instead, they must allow the mentee to choose a path that suits his or her needs.

Mentees' Motivation to Learn

Research has provided a fairly reliable body of knowledge about how adults learn. From review of the literature, one can gather that adults learn best when they are goal oriented and self-directed. They seek out learning experiences when facing life-changing events. New principals' success when facing the steep learning curve during the first critical years of service depends on their ability to meet external expectations, develop interpersonal relationships, turn obstacles or barriers into goals and positive outcomes, and maintain their self-esteem and sense of pleasure in the work they do. Mentors need to be attuned to the factors that impact their mentee's motivation to learn. They also must help their mentee visualize how to apply basic concepts to the job-embedded situations they face. Guiding the mutual reflection on experiences and new learning within a standards-based framework is important work for the mentor. Problems and experiences need to be anchored, analyzed, and understood in ways that encourage, rather than minimize, the mentee's willingness to take risks. And perhaps most important, mentors must have experience working with adult learners. Mentees bring previous knowledge and experience to any situation, and the mentor must be skilled at acknowledging, tapping into, and using prior and relevant knowledge while facilitating the active participation in and personalization of learning new skills and concepts.

What implication does the mentee's motivation to learn have for mentoring partnerships? First, mentees' learning will be enhanced when they play a key role in the identification of the experiences, issues, or problems to be discussed. Their desire to stay on top of the ever-increasing challenges of principalship will motivate them to ask questions, analyze, reflect, and learn while seeking applications for their unique situations. The mentor needs to recognize the mentee's readiness to learn and draw upon knowledge, experience, and best practices while guiding and enriching the self-directed learning of the mentee. And most importantly, the mentee's self-esteem is always on the line. Bitter disagreements, accusations, extensive focus on shortcomings, and mentor vs. mentee power struggles will lead to anguish and isolation for both participants.

A Brief Overview of the Research on Adult Learning

Mentors must understand not only how they best learn but also how their mentees react to, process, and gain new knowledge. Learning how the brain works by storing, retrieving, and acting upon new and prior knowledge is significant to understanding how adults learn. Principals are masters at helping young children formulate their new experiences, but adults learn differently. Mentors must have a comprehensive understanding of what is known about adult learning (Knowles, 1980):

- Adults learn best when they are involved in diagnosing, planning, implementing, and evaluating their own learning.
- The role of the facilitator is to create and maintain a supportive climate that promotes the conditions necessary for learning to take place.
- Adult learners have a need to be self-directing.
- Readiness for learning increases when there is a specific need to know.
- Life's reservoir of experiences is a primary learning resource; the life experiences of others enrich the learning process.
- Adult learners have an inherent need for immediacy of application.
- Adults respond best to learning when they are internally motivated to learn.

There are numerous books, articles, and Web sites with information about how adults learn:

The Adult Learner: The Definitive Classic in Adult Education and Human Resource Development (5th ed.), by Malcolm S. Knowles (1998), provides a clear review of the major educational theories of adult learning. It is a popular text in many college courses related to the subject.

Merriam and Caffarella's (1998) *Learning in Adulthood: A Comprehensive Guide* (2nd ed.) is an excellent textbook citing the most important contributions to adult learning from the 1990s.

Understanding and Facilitating Adult Learning: A Comprehensive Analysis of Principles and Effective Practice, by Stephen Brookfield (1991), details adult learning motives and processes, self-directedness, andragogy, the role of the facilitator, and learning in informal and formal settings. It is a good tool for any prospective mentor.

Mentors and mentees should read *30 Things We Know for Sure About Adult Learning,* by Ron and Susan Zemke (1984). Even though the article was written 20 years ago, the information is still accurate and relevant to mentoring partnerships.

Stephen Lieb's *Principles of Adult Learning* (1991) provides a concise description of four elements of adult learning that are key to every mentoring partnership. They are motivation, reinforcement, retention, and transference. Mentors, particularly, should review these elements. Mentors' awareness of their mentee's motivational interests and desired selfish benefits will help define and guide the partnership.

The American Association for Adult and Continuing Education publishes two periodicals. Information about *Adult Education Quarterly* and *Adult Learning* can be found by visiting their Web site at www.aaace.org. Visit http://adulted.about.com/ for resources with links to adult learning, continuing education, and coaching.

Finding a Mentor

It was midmorning of my first day as a principal. After eleven years teaching high school band followed by two years in fourth grade in a district where I knew almost everyone, I was now a principal. For the first time in my career, I was the new kid in town. Other than my secretary and custodians, I had yet to meet my staff. I was trying to make order of my office when a visitor appeared at my door. Little did I know that this visitor would become a mentor and lifelong friend.

Jonn Simmons had learned of my assignment and had come to welcome me to the district. He had taught at my school, lived down the street, and served as an elementary principal at another school in the district. I sensed immediately that I would like him, and I knew that his knowledge of my school, my staff, the community, district politics, and the organizational priorities of the principalship would be invaluable. His smile, sense of humor, and genuine concern for my welfare immediately set me at ease.

I'm sure Jonn never dreamed that his assistance with my learning would someday serve as a foundation for mentoring other principals. He was mentoring long before it was in vogue to do so. He became my friend, coach, teacher, guide, confidant, sounding board, encourager, and motivator. Little did I realize how he would influence my success during that first critical year as a leader.

Before he returned to his school, he made three suggestions. "I encourage you to join our state and national principals' associations—OAESA and NAESP. Make sure you join both. You'll soon appreciate the support you'll receive. Sign up now for the fall conference, and if you like, you can go with me. Now here is my phone number. Write it down. I'm just a phone call away anytime you have a question. Don't you ever hesitate to call. If you don't, I can't know how to help you." And with those memorable and insightful suggestions, he left.

I made many calls to Jonn that year. He helped me through many dilemmas similar to those of my protégés that constitute the case study of this book. His advice and support were always appropriate. His friendship has become priceless. And his introduction to the opportunities within the principals' associations started me on a professional journey that culminated with the presidency of NAESP. Jonn's mentoring, and that of many others, has shaped and enriched my personal and professional life.

Where does a beginning principal find a mentor? Most conveniently, for proximity, a mentor works within the same school district. But district sizes vary. Some mentors, as well as mentees, are more comfortable with individuals they do not work directly with as colleagues. Likewise, some prefer to mentor colleagues. Age, race, and gender may be factors that will impact some partnerships but not others. Some districts assign mentors and mentees. Many individuals seek out their own. State and national professional associations can assist by identifying prospective mentors and mentees and can facilitate connections. College, university, and professional development centers can also be resources. There is no prescribed or recommended method for mentor-mentee pairing. Both must be willing, committed, flexible, and able to accept one another as they are.

The initial moments of introduction are critical in the development of a principal mentoring partnership. First impressions are powerful. The partners quickly size each other up for compatibility, common interests, and goals. It takes time to develop trust and reduce levels of fear. The mentor must avoid coming on too strong and give the prospective mentee the opportunity to ask questions and become comfortable in the setting. Future meetings should be arranged. At all times, the mentor and mentee should understand that they are free to establish partnerships with others without negative consequences. When the introductory session outcomes are less than desired and expected, the mentor should reschedule and try again to establish a connection within a short period of time.

What are the qualities of an effective mentor? Effective mentors are individuals who understand balance and mutual interests. They respect the needs of their mentee. They are open and clearly communicate expectations. They are generous with their time. They accept their differences with the mentee and maintain focus on the objectives and outcomes of the partnership. They are trustworthy and maintain confidences. They provide straightforward feedback and, when necessary, can be brutally frank. But they counter those moments with compassion and understanding in pursuit of the highest levels of communication. Mentors are filled with passion for the principalship. They have pride in their work. The pride they develop from the mentoring partnership will propel their motivation and create the vitality in the relationship that will enrich the experience of the mentee. Effective mentors encourage risk taking. They are courageous and bold. They are ambitious. They openly share their extensive professional network with their mentee. They exemplify the best of administrative abilities, positive attitude, and aspirations. They love to learn and love their learners.

Shared Responsibility

What are the roles and responsibilities of the mentor and the mentee? Are there rules? No—roles and responsibilities, yes.

Mentors must set about quickly to create a sense of interdependence in the partnership, avoiding the mentee's sole dependence on the mentor. Nothing will limit the potential for mutual learning more. Both must assume responsibility for identifying learning objectives, expected outcomes, experiences to share, times to reflect, processes for sharing information, ways to criticize, plans for sharing successes, and the creation of a climate conducive to trust, respect, and acceptance.

Mentors must initiate regular contact with the mentee. But contacts should not always be mentor initiated. Mentees must never hesitate to call, e-mail, or communicate with their mentor when they have a question or concern. Both must be respectful of time and personal commitments. When meetings are scheduled, punctuality must be respected. Obligations and respect for each other's needs must become high priority items. Fear, especially from any kind of personal or professional retribution or hurt feelings, must be eliminated from the relationship. A balanced relationship with a focus on learning must always be evident to everyone.

How do certain people make a mentoring partnership with so many elusive components work and come together? They focus on the development of their interpersonal relationship first. They do so through their commitment to each other and by maintaining focus on their love for learning. They respect their similarities as well as their differences. They acknowledge different learning styles. They are intuitive learners capable of making their own rules and creating learning processes that work best for them. Through trial and error, they develop a structure for their mentoring partnership that allows appropriate pacing, contains adequate challenges, and achieves mutual outcomes. They share self-interests and a common vision. They love to learn as a team.

THE FOUR PHASES OF PRINCIPAL MENTORING

Lois Zachary, in her book *The Mentor's Guide*, describes four phases of any mentoring relationship, whether formal of informal:

Preparing

Negotiating

Enabling

Closure

These stages resonate through the mentoring process experienced by the authors of this book. What follows is an analysis of each phase in the central case study of this book, with a description of what happened in the partnership.

Preparing

Because both Dustin and Jeromey were teachers at West School and Paul was their principal, it was logical that they would ask for Paul to be their on-site facilitator while they completed administrative internships in cooperation with Ashland University professors. Team planning and preparation were necessary to meet the requirements of the internship. Some activities and assignments were completed individually, while others were shared experiences between Dustin and Jeromey guided by Paul. The primary shared activity was the development of a Blue Ribbon Schools application for their school. This required hours of data collection, reflection, and analysis of school programs, which was ultimately beneficial to all three principalships.

Once Dustin and Jeromey completed the requirements of the administrative internship, the team moved from academia to the real world of preparing for and acquiring the first principalship for each protégé. Both asked Paul if he would continue to teach and guide them in preparation for their career advancement.

Much of the preparatory phase involved talking and considering various questions, including

- What is the real motivation for wanting to become a principal?
- What are the advantages of and/or obstacles to seeking a principalship at an early age?
- What readiness skills need continued support, and what new objectives need to be learned while an aspiring principal?
- What advantages are there to both mentor and mentee in developing a partnership?
- What does each individual bring to the partnership and receive in the end?
- Are the participants compatible for developing an ongoing learning relationship?
- What time commitments are necessary and expected to create an effective partnership?
- What are the roles and expectations of the participants?
- What are the advantages and disadvantages of working as a threesome?

The preparatory phase occurred during the 2000–2001 school year while Dustin and Jeromey taught third grade after obtaining their master's degrees and certification. If we could relive history, we know now that while the questions above are important, it is better to devote adequate time to focusing on what is necessary for a solid partnership and developing the learning outcomes.

Negotiating

Negotiating the formation of a mentoring partnership is not an easy phase. It can be quite crucial to the partnership's success. The negotiating phase requires talk time to plan the learning goals, content, and desired outcomes of the partnership. It is also the time when a number of sensitive issues must be addressed. It is the critical time when many of the details of the relationship are discussed and worked out.

Much of the negotiating phase centers on discussion of the following topics:

- Confidentiality
- Trust
- Reliability
- Boundaries of the partnership
- Responsibilities
- Time commitments and expectations
- Accountability
- Identification and resolution of pet peeves
- Ability to deliver and accept criticism
- Level of commitment of participants
- Desire
- Maturity
- Character and ethics
- Establishment of learning objectives and outcomes

During the negotiating phase, there was common agreement and comfort with most of the details. However, many of the sensitive issues required individual private talk time and in-depth conversations. Personal hopes, aspirations, and goals were shared between protégé and mentor. We also discussed our frustrations. There was a series of informal tests that helped solidify our interpersonal relationship and respect for each other. And at all times the option remained to seek guidance and support elsewhere if the partnership appeared to be uncomfortable, cumbersome, or less than desirable for any participant.

During the negotiating phase, both the mentor and the mentee must talk about and become comfortable with process skills crucial for success in close personal relationships:

- Building and sustaining the personal relationship
- Networking with others
- Coaching
- Communication (listening, checking for understanding, openness, articulation)
- Encouragement
- Facilitation of learning (planning, designing, implementing, and evaluating)
- Goal setting
- Guiding (role modeling and reflection)
- Conflict management
- Problem solving
- Providing and receiving feedback
- Reflecting (consideration of learning for future action)

Again, it is crucially important to spend time focused on these process skills and what they mean for both mentor and protégés. Then mentors and mentees may revisit negotiation of these skills while in the enabling phase of the partnership.

Figure 1.1 contains examples of ways to develop the requisite mentoring skills.

Enabling

During the enabling phase, the implementation of mentoring activities occurs. The enabling phase requires more time to evolve naturally than any other.

Proximity was an important factor affecting the partnership of the authors. When Dustin became the first to acquire a principalship, despite being less than 30 minutes away he sensed that he was removed, isolated, and alone. Because of Jeromey's continued immediate access to a mentor at West School, his personal relationship continued to evolve, grow, and strengthen while Dustin's was strained by perceived distance. Dustin's enabling issues and activities quickly became different from considerations for Jeromey. It is a credit to both that potential competitive jealousies and personal insecurities did not sabotage the three-way partnership and interpersonal relationships. There were issues, lessons, and discussions that were tailored to fit the specific needs of each, while at other times learning was applicable to both.

Even though proximity has been an advantage for our partnership, each protégé responds differently. Dustin has been more hesitant

	Skill	Examples
1.	Building and sustaining the personal relationship	a. talk time focused on feelings b. talk about mentoring and personal experiences c. get to know each other d. periodically review and discuss needs e. social time together
2.	Networking with others	a. join professional associations b. attend state and national conference c. encourage involvement and leadership roles in local, state, and national professional associations d. model the development of contact networks e. discussion
3.	Coaching	a. fill knowledge gaps in a variety of "how to" situations b. observe performance on-site and identify learning needs c. "heads up" communiqués to alert protégés about deadlines and responsibilities d. identify ways to work smarter rather than harder
4	Communicating	a. schedule mentoring breakfasts b. phone conversations c. e-mails d. review staff bulletins e. observe speaking opportunities
5.	Encouraging	a. write notes, compliments, calls, praise, contacts, competition, listening
6.	Facilitating	a. share files, read books, share work samples, co-present at conferences
7.	Goal Setting	a. review personal goals and aspirations b. develop and critique professional goals and progress updates for contractual evaluation c. encourage building initiatives and professional development d. encourage advanced degree work
8.	Guiding	a. discuss, review options but do not tell protégé a specific way to do something b. listen, ask questions for clarity
9.	Conflict management	a. discuss conflict reaction characteristics and comfort levels b. model resolution skills c. listen, share, and guide as situations develop in schools with students, parents, and staff
10.	Problem solving	a. brainstorm, evaluate, model, reflect
11.	Providing and receiving feedback	a. evaluate oral and written communication b. review planning and implementation of programs
12.	Reflecting	a. personal talk time; debrief; share stories; collect data; document events, activities, and incidents b. adult learning

Figure 1.1   The Roles, Activities, and Skills of Mentoring

to initiate a contact when dealing with a problem. As a result, he has experienced stressful days and felt more isolated. He has learned that the protégé has as much responsibility to identify learning needs and initiate the phone call as the mentor.

In August 2003, the mentor and mentees became colleagues in the same district. There is frequent contact and communication between the district's nine elementary principals. More than ever, with cell phones the mentor is just a phone call away. The good mentor initiates contacts when he feels too much time has transpired without checking in.

During the enabling phase, Dustin and Jeromey have grown as our collaborative work has become intertwined, weaving together issues related to school management, instructional leadership, visioning, mentoring, and leading change within our community. We have become increasingly competitive and ambitious. We push and challenge each other and enjoy learning. We recognize that our interpersonal relationships are ever changing. We have made adjustments as the tugs and tears have developed. We share high standards and expectations.

The enabling phase continues as both protégés continue learning how to ask for assistance and receive, accept, and apply feedback, not only from their mentor but from a variety of other sources. We continue to share work and responsibilities between our neighboring and interconnected schools. Inevitably, things happen that test the viability of our mentoring partnership. These challenges would occur with or without our proximity. Because we have instinctively developed close personal relationships and trust each other, our partnership has persevered through

- District grapevine rumors and misinformation,
- Jealousy from colleagues,
- Personal attacks and affronts toward one or more of us,
- Mistakes and ineffective performance,
- Inaccurate assumptions of learned skill levels,
- Limitations of time and resources,
- Conflict between personal and professional time,
- Breakdowns in communication.

We have learned that we must periodically monitor the quality of our partnership and interaction. We reflect as a group or one-on-one. We have learned to acknowledge that there are certain courtesies that sustain our relationship, such as prompt return of phone calls, immediate attention to requests for information and assistance, recognition of successes, sharing, and initiation of contacts. We tweak when necessary and focus on how best to grow and focus on learning. We challenge each other to avoid apathy or cynicism. We monitor our interactions for stress and burnout. We help each other carry our burdens. Most of all, we work hard, but we also set aside time for social activities and the enjoyment of each other's company.

Closure

We recognize that closure of our mentoring partnership likely poses the greatest challenges. Experiences that each have brought to the partnership show that mentoring is an evolving process, and hopefully each of us will recognize the appropriate time for closure before we experience a bittersweet ending. Although we now assume that our personal bonds will remain rooted and strong for life, deep down we know that time and circumstances will likely cause things to be different than we anticipate. Closure has many emotional considerations, and we must work to avoid anxiety, fear, resentment, disappointment, or grief. Instead, we must focus on joy and accomplishment. We must always keep a focus on learning and growing. We will celebrate our successes and continue to share our stories. This book will become a testament to a very special shared moment in time, one filled with very satisfying and meaningful professional and personal experiences for each of us.

SHARING A VISION OF LEADERSHIP

For the principal mentor, one of the most challenging concepts is that of equipping and refining the mentee's vision of leadership. Being able to see the big picture, to understand the issues, and to influence people in ways that will enable them to change behaviors is an awesome undertaking. Some can envision what they would like their schools to become, but they cannot formulate a plan of action that will take them there. The importance of vision is often overlooked. Principals without vision are merely gatekeepers.

The National Association of Elementary School Principals (NAESP) publication *Leading Learning Communities: Standards for What Principals Should Know and Be Able to Do* defines standards for instructional leadership and quality in schools. A review of the indicators of quality is an excellent source of material for mentors as they engage their mentees in discussions of visioning. From the vignettes cited, mentees can take the bits and pieces that would work in their unique situation and adapt them to the vision of their school. To envision and create a quality school, most learners benefit from having multiple insights into what a quality school looks like. There is no reason to reinvent the wheel.

However, today's principals are challenged to know more than how to manage a school or be an instructional leader. They must have a vision and become masterful at simply *leading!*

John Maxwell's *Leadership 101* is a recommended read for every principal. His description of the stages and levels of leadership and their related myths should be helpful to every principal as he or she wrestles with visioning these elusive concepts. Maxwell identifies the five levels as:

1. Position

2. Permission

3. Production

4. People development

5. Personhood

Position Stage

When aspiring principals win a job, they enter the "position stage" of leadership. They have a title, but security in the position is based on talent. The unfortunate assume they have "made it" and begin basking in the power of the position, assuming that subordinates will willingly comply with all their decisions and ideas. It's not that simple, and school leadership doesn't work that way. Principals, like all leaders, must aspire to move to the higher levels. But one can't rush. Leaders can't skip a level. Principals can't move to the second level, permission, until they know their job description thoroughly, demonstrate awareness of the history of the organization, become a team player by relating the history of the organization to the people of the organization, accept responsibility, perform with consistent excellence, do more than expected, and offer creative ideas for change and improvement. People will not follow "positional" principals. School leaders must work to move higher.

Permission Stage

At the "permission level," people follow the principal because they want to. Principals can begin to lead toward a higher level because they have developed relationships with their staff. They devote time, energy, and focus on the followers' needs and desires.

To further advance to the third level, production, leaders in the permission stage demonstrate a genuine love for people, love people more than procedures, help those who work with them become more successful, see through other people's eyes, approach things from a position of "win-win" or choose not to do them, include others in the journey, and deal wisely with difficult people. People enjoy getting together just to get together.

Production Stage

The third level is where school staff begin to realize results from their work together. People follow the principal because of what he or she has done for the school.

People still like to get together, but they like to get together to accomplish a purpose—they are "results oriented." Most principals work at this level for long periods of time. They understand the importance of influence and the dues they must pay to earn it. To move to the fourth level, people development, they demonstrate mastery of initiating and accepting responsibility for growth and a development of a statement of purpose. They view their job description as an integral part of the statement of purpose. They develop accountability for results, know what to do to produce high returns, communicate the strategy and vision of the organization, and become a change agent. They understand timing and when to pick their battles. They become skilled at making the difficult decisions that will make a difference.

People Development Stage

At the people development stage, mentoring partnerships become a natural part of the principal's interests and responsibilities. Loyalty to the leader is highest when followers have personally grown through the mentorship of the leader. Principal mentors have the experience and influence to effectively guide their protégés, share their vast professional network, and maintain a way to keep in touch with everyone.

Principals who reach the people development stage of leadership realize that people are their most valuable asset. They place a priority on developing people and modeling for others. They pour their leadership efforts into the top 20% of their people—the "superstars"—exposing them to continual growth opportunities. They attract others who have ambition and share high expectations. Principals who are people developers, quite often found serving as mentors, surround themselves with an inner core of professionals that complements their leadership.

Personhood Stage

Most leaders never make it to "personhood." It is achievable, but it just takes longer than most people serve as a principal. The higher one moves through the stages, the longer it takes, and the higher one goes, the higher the level of commitment required. The higher one goes, the easier it is to lead! And leadership crumbles when a lower level is neglected.

Principals who attain the personhood level of leadership have followers that are loyal and sacrificial. They spend much of their time mentoring and molding leaders. They become consultants and quietly share what they've learned, amazed by their career journey. They have schools named in their honor.

How does any of this help an aspirant or a beginner gain a vision of the principalship? Maxwell's work outlines a map. Many must read and reflect to formulate their vision. Others need concrete examples and models. Still others will gain the most working closely one-on-one with a mentor. Whatever their learning style, beginning principals must understand that their chances for success can be profoundly influenced by identifying and working with a mentor, forming a close partnership, understanding how mentoring naturally evolves, tending diligently to their role as a mentee, understanding the progression of leadership, and focusing always on learning and growing toward a vision of leadership.

The books referenced above are recommended for both mentors and mentees. Reading each, in addition to this book, will help all mentoring participants establish a framework for creating a solid partnership, smoothly map the course of mentoring activities, understand the elements and levels of leadership, and create a vision of an effective school.

To develop positive successful people, look for the gold, not the dirt!

—John Maxwell, in *Developing
the Leaders Around You*

Part II

A Framework for Mentoring Objectives and Activities

From their multiple years in mentoring partnerships, the authors have developed a framework of 25 mentoring components including a "to do" list, each with "how to" options, assigned responsibilities, and learning objectives. This framework of suggestions is intended for use in a variety of ways and can be adapted to support each of the mentoring stages described in the previous chapter.

At the **preparation stage,** the list forms an overview of the process and a discussion starter between the partners as they preview their relationship and process.

At the **negotiating stage,** it can again be a list to return to as partners set goals and establish routines and personal protocols of engagement.

At the **enabling stage,** it becomes a document for self-monitoring, to monitor self-assessment and set new goals.

At the **closure stage,** it becomes a record to celebrate goals met and perhaps set new ones.

Suggestions for Mentoring Principals

	What Should Be Done	How to Do It	Responsibility	Desired Outcome
1.	Build a solid relationship.	Get to know things about the mentee. Both people need to enjoy time and feel comfortable with each other. Spend time connecting.	Mentor and mentee	Lifetime, trusting relationship.
2.	Focus on learning.	Know the general and specific requirements of managing and leading learners in a school. Focus on issues, not people. Solve problems rather than describe them in detail.	Mentor and mentee	Growth and more effective performance for both mentee and mentor.
3.	Establish regular meetings/contacts.	Arrange biweekly breakfasts, lunches, or informal meetings. Make regular phone contacts or visits. Determine locations for meetings. Be flexible.	Mentor and mentee	Regular contact that promotes sharing, time for reflection, and learning.
4.	Identify venues for communication.	Utilize face-to-face personal meetings, observations, telephone, e-mail, palm pilots and emerging technologies, and other means of contact with the mentee.	Mentor and mentee	Mutual agreement and understanding of the terms of communication for the partnership.
5.	Ask questions.	Inquire about the day-to-day work of the mentee. Ask questions about future planning, goals, and aspirations.	Mentor	Insights that will guide the direction and development of the partnership.
6.	Listen.	Allow time for the mentee to describe a situation and talk about sensitive or embarrassing issues. Be patient. Show empathy.	Mentor	Understanding of what is being said, how it is said, and what is not said.
7.	Guide. Don't tell.	Avoid giving answers. Assist the mentee in problem solving, understanding, and developing strategies that lead to new insights and meaningful learning.	Mentor	An independent, self-sufficient mentee.

	What Should Be Done	How to Do It	Responsibility	Desired Outcome
8.	Be constructive.	Be kind. Balance negative and positive comments. Critical feedback is crucial for growth.	Mentor	Growth and effective performance of the mentee.
9.	Share thoughts and feelings openly.	As the mentoring relationship progresses, this should become routine during meetings.	Mentor and mentee	Understanding of how each person perceives the environment.
10.	Maintain confidences.	Do not repeat information shared between mentor and mentee with any other person.	Mentor and mentee	Trust and respect among confidants.
11.	Check on the effectiveness of communication.	Review samples of mentee's writing (parent newsletters, staff communications, memos, letters). Observe the mentee while speaking in public.	Mentor	High levels of correctness, comfort, and effectiveness in written and oral communication.
12.	Be sensitive to the mentee's personal and learning needs.	Listen and give feedback. Ask personal questions when applicable. Be understanding.	Mentor and mentee	Balance between mentoring activities, work, home, and personal commitments.
13.	Reflect and talk about how the partnership is developing.	Mentoring meetings.	Mentor and mentee	Shared goals and expectations.
14.	Identify and discuss phases of mentoring.	Ongoing contacts, meetings, and discussions; reflection.	Mentor and mentee	Determine partnership guidelines, goals, outcomes, and predictable timelines.
15.	Share experiences.	Talk about positive as well as negative learning experiences. Share personal crucible experiences. Demonstrate that mentee's experiences are authentic and necessary for growth.	Mentor	Model learning by reflecting on professional experiences and career journey.

(Continued)

(Continued)

	What Should Be Done	How to Do It	Responsibility	Desired Outcome
16.	Learn together. Share professional contacts/network.	Invite the mentee to a professional conference or workshop. Share learning experiences. Make introductions, teach, and model the value of professional contacts.	Mentor	Collaborative bonds and mutual understanding. Expanded network including sharing mutual friends and contacts.
17.	Don't become overbearing and dominant in the relationship.	Avoid dictating choices, controlling behavior, and determining mentee's needs and values.		Balance and comfort in the partnership.
18.	Learn to deal with conflict.	Identify conflict management techniques and personal styles for dealing with conflict. Recognize that conflict is natural and can be good.	Mentor and mentee	Ability to resolve differences focused on issues rather than personalities.
19.	Look for stress build-up.	Observe physical mannerisms, health, attitude, and actions of the mentee. Share anxieties and concerns.	Mentor	Reduce worry and stress for the mentee.
20.	Establish goals.	Set high expectations for yourself and reflect frequently.	Mentor and mentee	Direction and aspirations.
21.	Learn about levels of leadership.	Reading, reflecting, sharing.	Mentor and mentee	Awareness of the importance of influence in a career path.
22.	Distinguish between management and instructional leadership activities.	Reflecting, reading *Leading Learning Communities: Standard for What Principals Should Know and Be Able to Do.*	Mentor and mentee	Balance, delegation, focus on improving learning.
23.	Model best practices.	Stay on top of your field. Know the issues. Share technical expertise. Know how to access the latest information. Be current. Be positive and progressive.	Mentor	Effective principal performance.

	What Should Be Done	How to Do It	Responsibility	Desired Outcome
24.	Appreciate cultural, race, and gender differences.	Respect diversity—expect adversity. Talk about differences. Acknowledge ethics and improper levels of interaction, contact, and closeness of mentoring partnership.	Mentor and mentee	Establishment of ethics and elimination of improper behavior.
25.	Plan for closure.	Avoid anxiety, resentment, or surprise. Anticipate the end of the partnership. Encourage mentee to expand and seek other forms of support in additional partnerships with other mentors.	Mentor and mentee	A natural evolving process. Closure that is amenable to both participants. Mutual reaping of the benefits of learning through mentoring.

Some of the suggestions are clearly stage-specific. Others, like modeling best practices, are ongoing throughout. The list of mentoring components will be more useful if the partners use it interactively. A few suggestions for this follow.

- Duplicate this list every week, date it, discuss it together and highlight areas of concentration.
- The mentor can duplicate it periodically, date it, and choose three mentoring suggestions. Self-assess around them in a mentoring journal and list some action steps for moving forward.
- The mentee can duplicate it and footnote selected items to identify experiences that promoted professional growth or may be linked to specific portfolio-appropriate documentation.

Whatever their learning style, beginning principals must understand that their future chances for success can be profoundly influenced by identifying and working with a mentor, forming a close partnership, understanding how mentoring naturally evolves, tending diligently to their role as a mentee, understanding the progression of leadership, and focusing always on learning and growing.

—Paul G. Young

Part III

Sample Agendas for Mentoring Breakfasts

Effective principals know how to run effective meetings. With that in mind, mentors should model good meeting facilitation skills for their protégés and develop an agenda for formal mentoring sessions. Each mentoring partnership will be as different as the individuals involved, and so will the agendas. However, it is important to structure these meetings meaningfully while also leaving room to include the "teachable moment." Those presented here as models are developed along two simultaneous threads: the natural sequence of events and demands presented by the school calendar, and attention to standards for principals as articulated by NAESP. A sample agenda worksheet that can and should be adapted as necessary is found at the end of this chapter.

Mentors will find NAESP's *Leading Learning Communities: Standards for What Principals Should Know and Be Able to Do* to be an excellent guide as they work with protégés to create and support quality in schools. The reader will note the standards are referenced in each agenda as appropriate:

1. **Leadership** — Lead schools in a way that places student and adult learning at the center.

2. **Vision** — Set high expectations and standards for the academic and social development of all students and the performance of adults.

3. **Student Learning** — Demand content and instruction that ensure student achievement of agreed-upon academic standards.

4. **Adult Learning** — Create a culture of continuous learning for adults tied to student learning and other school goals.

5. **Data and Decision Making** — Use multiple sources of data as diagnostic tools to assess, identify, and apply instructional improvement.

6. **Community Engagement** — Actively engage the community to create a shared responsibility for student and school success.

Each chapter of *Leading Learning Communities* contains self-assessments to be used throughout the school year. These can be helpful tools for mentors and protégés as they focus on their shared learning and development of leadership skills.

Mentors and protégés will develop a special bond. Many become very close friends and enjoy spending time together. But because principals are busy individuals, it is beneficial, particularly at the outset, to carve time from packed schedules to be with each other in ways other than formal meetings. Regardless, to structure the partnership it is helpful to have a predetermined reason to meet or topics to discuss. Both mentor and protégé should contribute those ideas. Failure to adequately plan and prepare often results in limited outcomes, and over time, both mentor and protégé will see less value in meeting and learning together.

What follows are sample agendas from mentoring breakfasts during the 2002–2003 mentoring school year. Always, each participant was allowed to present a pressing item that became a priority when necessary. In these cases, the agenda was shortened or postponed. Demonstrating how to balance leadership and management responsibilities and recognizing when to capture the teachable moment are important skills for a mentor to teach a protégé. At the same time, it is important for the mentor to provide a structure that is visible to the mentee, always surfacing the connection between both identified agenda items and immediate challenges with professional standards.

The agendas that follow are both personal to the authors and general to the process. Some of the personal elements have been kept as a way to indicate how to incorporate needs, strengths, or opportunities that individuals bring to the process.

Mentors and protégés must devote time to getting to know each other and mutually agree upon the structure of mentoring meetings. Develop an agenda that works for you. Keeping an agenda will help the mentor and the protégé document and reflect on the progress of their partnership.

It is beneficial to precede the first agenda-based meeting with more informal contact such as unstructured get-to-know-you meetings, phone calls, lunch, and social events. Plan a round of golf, watch a ball game, or attend a professional conference together.

Beginning each meeting by sharing experiences of the week can be helpful. By listening, the mentor can perceive immediate needs and determine ways to better support the protégé. The protégé will feel validated when issues are heard and given a response. But both protégé and mentor must guard against monopolizing time and sidetracking the direction of the meeting. Should an issue arise that requires immediate attention, the agenda should be changed with mutual agreement or another meeting established to deal with pressing issues.

The IAT (Intervention Assistance Team) discussion (Standards 1 and 2, Leadership and Vision) on the November 9 agenda focused on the protégé's learning and articulation of the meeting process, interaction with staff, and the development of good academic and behavioral interventions.

Don't forget to add humor. Collect the stories. Share them with others. Mentors and protégés who laugh together will stay together.

Student learning is an obvious reason for promoting spelling bees, but the discussion in the January 11, 2003 agenda focused more on the principal's conceptualization of the responsibilities related to engaging the community. Spelling bees can be a vehicle for encouraging parents to become meaningfully involved in their school and their child's learning. But for the protégé who must organize a local school event for the first time—especially where a valued, successful bee has been the norm—the wise mentor should encourage and guide through envisioning various leadership activities. Spelling bees are not to be taken lightly. The principal must be able to anticipate problems before they develop. Good planning is essential. Public speaking and communication, decision making, and creating a positive school climate are key.

The January 25, 2003 meeting was scheduled to further discuss issues related to management versus instructional leadership. However, between meetings, one protégé had encountered an act of vandalism at his school. He needed to share his actions and feelings and an authentic learning opportunity became apparent.

It is also important to share and vent, for both protégé and mentor. District politics, parent, and staff problems are ever-present and need to be openly discussed throughout mentoring partnerships. Confidentiality and trust must be established at high levels.

Mentors and protégés can identify many topics to share with colleagues at professional conferences. The discoveries and affirmations in preparation for an NAESP presentation are a source of adult learning for the protégés and the mentor.

February can be brutal. Adults and students alike begin feeling the effects of cabin fever. Principals are no different. Routine events can drag people down. State testing follows in March. Tension levels are high.

Through professional networking and sharing, principals learn to support each other. During stressful times, such as midwinter, mentors and protégés can really appreciate their time together. Focus on people. Share and learn with other adults, not in isolation. A principal's decision to spend time learning from a colleague is an investment in good physical and mental health.

History books will soon document the events of the invasion of Iraq, but during our March 15, 2002 meeting the events were real and unfolding. Adults and students were on edge, fearful of further acts of terrorism. It became a wise investment of time to allow protégés and mentor to share innermost thoughts, fears, and questions before beginning a week as leaders of schools. The answers still were lacking, but the mutual support became invaluable.

The April 5, 2003 agenda reflects the pileup of events and responsibilities that come with spring. Specifics will vary from school to school, but for all principals, this is a busy and challenging time of the school year.

The April 26, 2003 agenda contained items related to professional networking, adult learning, and community engagement for the mentor and protégés to discuss and reflect upon. Additionally, there were numerous topics that involved planning for the end of one school year and preparing for the next. The effective mentor integrates discussions of the "little things" and guides the protégé to reflect about planning and conceptualization of upcoming events and activities (vision).

Professional development activities related to a state Access Grant were in full swing at the time of the May 17, 2003 meeting. Learning was current, real, and meaningful for the mentor and protégés. The mentor was wrestling with ways to improve the IAT process. Throughout the discussion, the mentor attempted to model effective adult learning and visioning.

With an approaching end of the year, many items need to be shared. Wrapping up a school year can be an overwhelming time for new principals, and the advice and guidance of a mentor can prove invaluable and prevent errors.

As the school year progressed, even though there continued to be common topics in the agendas, the protégés gained tremendous confidence in their roles. The elements of mentoring became less important to participants as the shared time gradually evolved to collaboratively planning activities and professional development opportunities for each school. This evolution occurred naturally and has developed into a form of collegiality that can continue indefinitely.

Mentoring Breakfast

September 12, 2002
Bob Evans Restaurant
7:30 a.m.

Agenda

Item	Standard	Person	Time	Outcome/s
Share experiences of the week — reflect	4 – Adult Learning	Everyone	10 minutes	Reflection, advice, support, and sharing
Staff observation, evaluation schedules, pre-observation conference	3 – Student Learning	Everyone	15 minutes	Review of processes, expectations, and timelines; assure that students are being taught to standard and learning; certified vs. classified staff
Proficiency testing	5 – Data & Decision making	Everyone	5 minutes	Review of test security precautions; 4th grade October reading test administration; benchmarking student progress
Parent-teacher conferences	6 – Community engagement	Everyone	5 minutes	Review of planning; encouraging parents to be involved
Sharing of files	1 – Leadership	Everyone	5 minutes	Shared access and connection to building servers, sharing of staff bulletins; gathering ideas from each other
Veterans' Day assembly	6 – Community engagement	Paul	5 minutes	Tips for scheduling, conducting an assembly
What can I be doing to assist you?	4 – Adult Learning	Everyone	5 minutes	Identification of needs, assistance and mentoring

Mentoring Breakfast

November 9, 2002
Bob Evans Restaurant
7:30 a.m.

Agenda

Item	Standard	Person	Time	Outcome/s
Share experiences of the week – reflect	4 – Adult Learning	Everyone	10 minutes	Reflection, advice, support, and sharing
Intervention Assistance Team (IAT) Leadership	1 & 2 – Leadership & Vision	Dustin, Jeromey	20 minutes	Ideas for enhancing leadership, sharing of concerns and/or success Articulation of team progress to improve student achievement
Planning for the month	4 – Adult Learning	Everyone	10 minutes	Learning from each other
Reflection topics (select) • Paperwork • Computer work • Out and about listening/talking with people • Planning • Reading • Instructional leadership • Managing • Disciplining	4 – Adult Learning	Everyone	30 minutes	Increased learning, sharing, discussion, opportunity to think together
Tell a particularly funny story about your school		Everyone	5 minutes	Humor and fun
What can I be doing to assist you better?	4 – Adult Learning	Paul	?	Ideas and direction for assistance and future mentoring sessions

Mentoring Breakfast

January 11, 2003
Bob Evans Restaurant
7:30 a.m.

Agenda

Item	Standard	Person	Time	Outcome/s
Share experiences of the week; open time to present ideas, vent, question, etc. – Reflect	4 – Adult Learning	Everyone	10 minutes	Reflection, advice, support, and sharing
Spelling Bee Preparations	6 – Community Engagement	Dustin, Jeromey	10 minutes	Planning for local events at schools; review of details of preparations
Discussion topics (select) • Handling stress • District politics • Managing vs. leading • Observations/ evaluations	1 – Leadership	Everyone	30 minutes	Increased learning, sharing, discussion
Describe something that has happened in your school of which you are most proud	4 – Adult Learning	Everyone	5 minutes	Humor and fun
What can I be doing to assist you better?	4 – Adult Learning	Paul	?	Direction for assistance and mentoring

Mentoring Breakfast

January 25, 2003
Bob Evans Restaurant
7:30 a.m.

Agenda

Item	Standard	Person	Time	Outcome/s
Share experiences of the week – Reflect	4 – Adult Learning	Everyone	10 minutes	Reflection, advice, support, and sharing
School Break-in	1 & 4 – Leadership, Adult Learning	Jeromey	10 minutes	Share learning, feelings, perceptions of others of handling the situation, plans to avoid future problems
Visioning	2 – Vision	Everyone	10 minutes	Understanding of how to visualize your school and its continuous improvement
Reflection topics (select) • Student problems • Parent problems • Staff problems • Union problems	1 – Leadership	Everyone	30 minutes	Increased learning, sharing, discussion
Planning for NAESP Presentation, April 2003, West School, "When the Bad Becomes the Good"	4 & 5 – Adult Learning and Data and Decision Making	Everyone	5 minutes	Review of program outline and individual expectations
What can I be doing to assist you better?	4 – Adult Learning	Paul	?	Direction for assistance and mentoring

Mentoring Breakfast

February 8, 2003
Bob Evans Restaurant
7:30 a.m.

Agenda

Item	Standard	Person	Time	Outcome/s
Share experiences of the week – Reflect	4 – Adult Learning	Everyone	10 minutes	Reflection, advice, support, and sharing
Spelling Bee – Reflect	4 – Adult Learning	Dustin, Jeromey	10 minutes	Share experiences of the process, challenges, and operation of a building event, confidence, and improvement for future activities
Share your biggest current frustration	4 – Adult Learning	Dustin, Jeromey	10 minutes	Support, ideas, and guidance
How are your handling stress?	4 – Adult Learning	Everyone	10 minutes	Sharing and support
Reflection topics (select) • Parent problems • Student problems • Staff problems building/ district • Proficiency testing • Other	4 – Adult Learning	Everyone	30 minutes	Increased learning, sharing, discussion
Staffing for 2003–2004	1 – Leadership	Everyone	5 minutes	Information, heads-up awareness of processes and procedures
What can I be doing to assist you better?	4 – Leadership	Paul	?	Direction for assistance and mentoring

Mentoring Breakfast

March 15, 2002
Bob Evans Restaurant
7:30 a.m.

Agenda

Item	Standard	Person	Time	Outcome/s
Share experiences of the week – Reflect	4 – Adult Learning	Everyone	10 minutes	Reflection, advice, support, and sharing
Gulf War Planning	1 and 4 – Leadership and Adult Learning	Everyone	10 minutes	Ideas and plans for leading schools through times of televised war with Iraq; possible terrorist reactions
Access Grant	1 – Leadership	Everyone	10 minutes	Review of plans and details for working with consultants in upcoming workshop
OAESA Aspiring Principals Workshop	4 – Adult Learning	Dustin	5 minutes	Reflection and sharing of panel presentation highlights
Discussion topics (select) • Paperwork reduction • Budget cuts • Enrollment for next year • Lock down drills • Staffing for next year • Sharing school newsletters, bulletins	1 – Balancing Leadership and Management	Everyone	30 minutes	Increased learning, sharing, discussion
What are you doing for professional growth?	4 – Adult Learning	Everyone	5 minutes	Share readings, inservice opportunities, learning
What can I be doing to assist you better?	4 – Adult Learning	Paul	?	Direction for assistance and mentoring

Mentoring Breakfast

April 5, 2003
Bob Evans Restaurant
7:30 a.m.

Agenda

Item	Standard	Person	Time	Outcome/s
Share experiences of the week – Reflect	4 –Adult Learning	Everyone	10 minutes	Reflection, advice, support, and sharing
NAESP Presentations	4 – Adult Learning	Everyone	10 minutes	Share experiences: how to add music to PowerPoint presentation – Dustin to teach Paul
Share your biggest current frustration	4 – Adult Learning	Dustin, Jeromey	10 minutes	Support, ideas, and guidance
Proficiency Testing	1 & 5 – Leadership and Data and Decision Making	Everyone	10 minutes	Reflection on the process
Discussion topics (select) • Spring break activities • NAESP convention • IAT processes • Presidential academic and fitness awards • Web sites • Gulf War adaptations	4 – Adult Learning	Everyone	30 minutes	Increased learning, sharing, discussion
Spring Carnivals	4 – Learning	Everyone	5 minutes	Information, heads-up awareness of processes and procedures
What can I be doing to assist?	4 – Adult Learning	Paul	?	Direction for assistance and mentoring

Mentoring Breakfast

April 26, 2003
Bob Evans Restaurant
7:30 a.m.

Agenda

Item	Standard	Person	Time	Outcome/s
Share experiences of the week – Reflect	4 – Adult Learning	Everyone	10 minutes	Reflection, advice, support, and sharing
Review of SWAP (Supervision with a Principal) Program	6 – Community Engagement	Everyone	10 minutes	Share experiences of the process, challenges, and opportunities to connect with community leaders; ideas to improve the program for next year
Breakfast in the Classroom	2 – Vision	Jeromey, Paul	10 minutes	Sharing ideas with Paul for 2003–2004 that articulate need for new program
Access Grant Planning	2 – Leadership	Everyone	10 minutes	Clarification of expectations for staff learning
Reflection topics (select) • Planning daily, weekly, monthly • Discipline plans, activities • Doctoral program at Nova Southeastern University • Changes for next year? (PTO, schedules, duties, etc.) • Other	4 – Adult Learning	Everyone	30 minutes	Increased learning, sharing, reflection, ideas, discussion
Do you ever feel overwhelmed? What is foremost on your mind?	4 – Adult Learning	Everyone	10 minutes	Reflection
What can I be doing to assist you better?	4 – Adult Learning	Paul	?	Direction for assistance and mentoring

Mentoring Breakfast

May 17, 2003
Bib's Restaurant
7:30 a.m.

Agenda

Item	Standard	Person	Time	Outcome/s
Reflect on positive and negative experiences of the week	4 – Adult Learning	Everyone	10 minutes	Reflection, advice, support, and sharing
Access Grant	4 – Adult Learning	Everyone	10 minutes	Reflect and share experiences and feelings from workshop, identify weakness of preparation, planning for improvement
IAT Process Changes	1 & 2 – Leadership and Vision	Everyone	10 minutes	Developing ideas and plans from the Access Grant consultant (Margaret Searle) and implementing in our three schools in 2003–2004
• End of the year planning • Check out memo • Inventories • Keeping a lid on student discipline	1 & 4 – Balancing Management and Leadership; Adult Learning	Paul	10 minutes	Support, ideas, and guidance; sharing of experience
Reflection topics (select) • Parent problems • Student problems • Staff problems building/district • Other	4 – Adult Learning	Everyone	30 minutes	Increased learning, sharing, discussion
What can I be doing to assist you better?	4 – Adult Learning	Paul	?	Direction for assistance and mentoring

Mentoring Breakfast

May 31, 2003
Bob Evans Restaurant
7:30 a.m.

Agenda

Item	Standard	Person	Time	Outcome/s
Share experiences of the week – Reflect	4 – Adult Learning	Everyone	10 minutes	Reflection, advice, support, and sharing
Access Grant	1 & 2 – Leadership and Vision	Everyone	15 minutes	Plan for gaining further support; determination of consultant's status, delegation of summer activities and future preparations
Staffing process/Room Assignments	1 – Leadership	Everyone	20 minutes	Reflection, strategies for improving the process, events, and activities
Chess tournament	6 – Community Engagement	Everyone	5 minutes	Coverage at school and appearance
Social Event		Everyone	2 minutes	Determination of possible dates; networking/bonding activity
Copying CDs to computer	4 – Adult Learning	Dustin, Paul		Music for PowerPoint presentation
What can I be doing to assist you at the end of the year; activities during summer two week extended service period?	4 – Adult Learning	Paul	5 minutes	Direction for assistance and mentoring

Mentoring Breakfast

Date:
Place:
Time:

Agenda Worksheet

Item	Standard	Person	Time	Outcome/s
Sharing activity – Reflect	4 – Adult Learning	Protégé, Mentor	10 minutes	Reflection, advice, support, and sharing
What can I be doing to assist you better?	4 – Adult Learning	Mentor		Direction for assistance and mentoring

Part IV

Job-Embedded Real Time Mentoring

Stories of Mentoring and Lessons Learned, With Reflections From the Mentor and Mentees

---

The stories that follow exemplify the kind of mentoring that takes place around specific events, issues, and crises of various magnitudes. As noted in the earlier discussion of adult learning, it's often the lessons taken from these job-embedded and immediately necessary mentoring interactions that have the most lasting value. Some of the topics here are clearly of enough importance that they could migrate to a formal agenda as well. However, for new mentors, these stories are offered to foreshadow the kinds of crises through which they may need to support their mentees, and to show ways to provide that support. For new principals or mentees reading this book, it is hoped that these stories will provide reassurance that all new principals feel cracks in their confidence at times. Even as they grow in assurance they will, throughout their careers, need to turn sometimes to a mentor or colleague to support them through a decision making process or formation of an action plan.

The reader will notice that the focus of many of the stories is management based. Still, many others center around adult learning, both of the protégé and the mentor. Intertwined through all the stories are subthemes of creating a vision for an effective school. The beginning principal must always be aware of the needs of student and adult learners and strive to create a culture of high expectations, quality instruction, and continuous improvement. And to achieve success, a balance between management and instructional leadership must be attained. The wise mentor makes time to assure that the protégés' solid management practices and style are deeply rooted before nurturing instructional leadership. The principal can't effectively lead instruction if the buses don't run, the students misbehave, the cafeteria doesn't serve good meals, the office is disorganized, the school is dirty or cluttered, or irate parents consume inordinate amounts of time. As you will see, the scenarios that follow document two beginning principals' experiences as they worked to master myriad management tasks, create a vision for their schools, interact with their school communities, and become leaders in ways that always place student and adult learning at the center. The mentor attempted to guide and nurture in each situation, realizing the immediacy of adult learning. At all times, the mentor and protégés recognized the value of a strong partnership as it impacted care of their organizations, themselves, and their professional growth.

The stories are grouped by categories as they occurred during the phases of mentoring: preparing, negotiating, enabling, and closure. The reader will notice more appear in the enabling phase—the time of implementation—than others. This phase is when the work gets done and adults learn most. The stories are structured so that they begin with the mentor's recollection and observations regarding the lessons learned, followed by the reflections of the mentee.

PREPARING

MY RIGHT AND LEFT HANDS

By coincidence, Jeromey and Dustin became third grade teaching partners during the 2000–2001 school year. Dustin was the newest addition to our staff. I hadn't anticipated the opportunities that lay ahead for our mentoring partnerships. Both were enrolled in graduate programs and working toward their administrative certification. Both asked if I would serve as their on-site coordinator for the administrative internship. As they became involved in many projects, their contributions to our school were invaluable. They became my right and left hands.

Dustin and Jeromey responded positively to my high expectations and drive. As a threesome, we worked together on many projects. We often worked until late in the evening. I was testing their commitment and ability to juggle many demands. Their college professors were impressed with the output from their internship assignments and their learning and growth. It was exciting to watch them develop and mature and set about advocating their advancement within the district and elsewhere. Having their assistance, listening to their feedback, and challenging them past their comfort zones became exciting. Knowing their eyes and ears were focused on everything that I said and did forced me to reevaluate my actions and beliefs. I concentrated on my own learning as much as theirs. I strived to become their best role model. I acquired a new interest in the principalship. Influencing and developing people became an awesome responsibility and enhanced my interest in leadership. I received as much or more than I gave. The year we spent together in the same school remains one of the most memorable of my career.

Would I recommend to others that they work with two young protégés simultaneously? As can be imagined, there were many potential pitfalls: unfair comparisons, confidentiality issues, evaluation sensitivities, equitable distribution of assignments, competition for the same principalships, and the potential "two against one" complexities due to our generational difference. Having great respect for both, when they began interviewing in neighboring districts for the same position, I dreaded what I would say when asked for personal references. I could identify strengths and weaknesses for each—fortunately I was never put in an uncomfortable position. As they are competitive individuals, my worst fear was that in pursuing the same jobs one would be hired and I would have to console the other.

As it happened, both spent a summer interviewing together in several districts. Those experiences were good, although they seemed always to lose out in the final interviews to an older candidate with more experience. But a week before school began, when most principalships in the area were filled, a position opened in a neighboring district. Dustin's grandparents lived in the small community, he had attended church there, and he wanted the job. When the superintendent called for the reference check, I was pleased to assure her that Dustin could do the job, despite his young age.

A week later, Jeromey's offer arrived. But classes were scheduled to begin the next day, and he was denied release from the district. Disappointed, he remained at our school as a teacher and my right-hand man, becoming my substitute when I was away fulfilling NAESP responsibilities. He became the heir apparent to serve as the interim principal of West School the upcoming year when I was scheduled to leave to serve as President of NAESP. But by March, the principal of North School resigned to become an assistant superintendent in another district. Jeromey interviewed for both the North and West positions, and was named as the new principal of North School. Both were now principals at 27 years of age.

Worried about a suitable interim principal for West School, I convinced Dustin to apply and the superintendent to consider him for hiring. I was pleased when it all transpired; we are now colleagues. When I return to West School after serving as President, we will serve principalships in schools less than two miles apart. Exciting times are ahead.

Would I recommend working with two protégés at the same time? Probably not. My situation required that I did. Both had the opportunity to seek a mentor elsewhere, and both do consult with other people. We have had to work to develop and maintain a strong, sensitive, trusting relationship, one-to-one as well as within our threesome. It hasn't always been easy or worked well. We continue to develop, learn, grow, and solidify a strong partnership. There are times when I work one-on-one, others where we share openly our joys and frustrations as a group. When they do not meet my expectations, I risk losing their trust when I am critical. The two against one scenario is always potentially present. They pick and choose when to challenge their mentor out of respect for their elder and risk of conflict. Our relationship is valuable; we agree to work hard to protect and continuously improve it. I have been blessed to have support from my right- and left-hand protégés. I am invigorated as their mentor. The immense influence and responsibility I have in shaping their careers requires me to commit to and work toward high expectations just as much as each of them.

Lesson Learned

Don't assume that mentoring must always be a private, one-to-one partnership. Talk about options when there might be two or more mentees to work with at the same time. Challenge your assumptions, biases, and stereotypes. Take risks. Allow each learner to shape the structure of the partnership and have confidence in one another's abilities to develop a close interdependence and strong relationship. Things have a way of working out for the best!

Mentors will gain as much or more from the partnership as the mentees.

Adults learn best when they have immediate needs. There is power in sharing and reflecting with trusted friends. The protégé presenting the issue learned most from the feedback because of the need. The mentor and observer also learned from the opportunity to reflect.

THE NEXT GENERATION

When Jeromey and Dustin both talked with me about their desire to become principals at their young ages, at first, like others, I questioned their experience level and capabilities. But their desire was evident. Both had the "fire in the belly." Waiting additional years before leaving the classroom might have had some advantages, but it became clear to me that they were ready. I think they both realized they would miss valuable opportunities to share this special partnership if they waited. They expected me to retire!

Despite their efforts and on-the-job performance, it is difficult to downplay their youthful appearance and lack of experience. Many older and more experienced people don't easily accept their youthfulness. Some take advantage of them. Jeromey was stung recently when he learned from a reliable source that another colleague had made comments about his being "green." It has been an ongoing campaign for both to earn people's respect. It is difficult to gain credibility. It takes time. Both have followed principals old enough to be their parents. Both are among the youngest people in their schools. I am sure they can relate to other biases and discrimination such as gender and race.

It is a credit to the leadership of this school district that it saw their potential and took a risk with two young principals. The rewards will come within a few years. Perhaps if there hadn't been recognition of the mentoring partnership and the support they would have, the outcome would be different. Regardless, they are who they are, working as hard as they can, and doing well. It won't be long until the pups of today become the big dogs. And our district will have been the beneficiary.

Lesson Learned

People can enter the principalship at any age and experience success or failure. To ensure success, beginning principals need a mentor. Beyond that, the beginning principal must show desire, dedication, and commitment. He or she must continually do what is right for children, speak to the issues, and lead. No matter one's age, credibility comes with proven performance, and that simply requires time and experience. Adults who want to learn will surround themselves with structures that best support the immediacy of their needs. Mentoring will support the adult learning needs of beginning principals.

Memo to Dustin

This memo was written for Dustin as he began his first principalship. It is applicable to all beginning principals.

M E M O

TO: Dustin
FROM: Paul
RE: Tips to Assure Your Success

You've made me extremely proud as you prepared and succeeded in securing your first job as principal. You are embarking on the most noble of careers, and I am here for you anytime you need my help. When you have time, read the following tips, internalize as many as you can, and you'll make it. I am only a phone call away, and as you've heard me say before, there are no foolish questions.

1. Join your local, state, and national professional associations TODAY!

2. Don't be the last person at school or the first to leave. The opposite is probably better.

3. Check your mail and e-mail the first thing at work and regularly throughout each day.

4. Return all phone messages before you leave for the day.

5. Call parents and tell them good things—then when the bad comes, they can accept it better.

6. Write notes regularly—daily. Buy several packs of "thank you" and "congratulations" note cards. Focus on your staff, students, parents, and your community.

7. Read the local newspaper and clip articles to send to people in your school district.

8. Treat your secretary, custodians, bus drivers, and food service personnel well. They can make or break you.

9. Planning ahead is essential for success. Write a weekly staff bulletin to keep everyone informed of school activities.

10. Memorize names of everyone as quickly as you can. Priority item!

11. Use a computer to work smarter rather than harder.

12. Organize your office files. Document, document, document! Take time to read each day—the newspaper, key Web sites, professional journals, personal interests.

13. Keep a journal and write about your experiences.

14. Laugh a lot and show a sense of humor.

15. Avoid the gossip in the lounge and the district grapevine news. Hard to do!

16. Visit at least three classrooms each day.

17. Attend professional conferences and network. Your building can survive without you for one day.

18. Explore and become knowledgeable about every aspect of your physical plant.

19. If you can't think of something nice to say, don't say anything at all.

20. Buy time. Not every decision requires immediate response.

21. Be visible in your school, the district, and the community. Eat lunch with the students. Attend the football game this Friday night. Be a cheerleader for your school.

22. Tell the truth.

23. Focus most of your attention and energy on improving instructional leadership. Be a leader.

24. Always dress first class, think first class, act first class!

25. Put my phone number on speed dial.

Best wishes for a smooth school opening! You'll love being a principal, and I'll always be here to help!

Your mentor, colleague, and friend,

Paul Young

Two Different Worlds

In Jeromey's second interview for his initial teaching position, I asked him to sing "Mary Had a Little Lamb." I doubted that a "jock" would or could sing in front of me, let alone lead the singing of a group of second graders while introducing good literature. But he met my challenge and won my respect on the spot.

As Jeromey gained experience at West School, I always hoped he would see and understand the value of and the role played by the arts in our school transformation. Now as a principal, together we experience the battles to protect the integrity of the arts programs in our schools. I am pleased to consider him my ally in this ongoing effort. I hope his life, as well as those in his school, will always be enriched by experiences in the arts.

Mentee Reflection: Jeromey

Growing up, I loved the competitiveness that athletics offered. Involved in baseball, track, football, weight training, and wrestling, I learned quickly what it takes to earn a spot on the team, win a championship, and make a mark in history. My life revolved around competition and hard work.

When it came to socializing, I hung out with people that were like me—competitive and athletic. I was always aware that other groups and activities existed but never really took the time to learn about them. You might say that I was a typical jock and liked to hang out with other jocks.

It wasn't until I met Paul that I learned the importance of other curricular areas and how they relate to education. Paul had earlier experience as a high school band director and was a huge supporter of arts in education. Because of my sports background and a lack of support for the arts in my high school, it was hard for me to realize that a band concert was as important as a Friday night football game.

Paul taught me how important music was in his life and how I should support the arts in my school. To be honest, I had never attended a band concert until I started my teaching career in Lancaster. If it hadn't been for Paul's influence, I probably wouldn't have realized the importance of supporting the students in my school in their desire to study music.

Students who played in the band in my high school were considered nerds and put down. They were not really part of the "in" crowd. It was because of Paul's influence on my life and his love for music that I now can understand the importance of the arts. I see how they can improve the culture of my school. And I know that students aren't better or worse because of an activity they choose, but instead, they become unique and talented because of their hard work—no matter the activity.

Lesson Learned

School principals have a responsibility to offer a broad array of activities and learning experiences for all students. Sports, the arts, and a variety of co-curricular activities are a necessity in quality schools. The principal's involvement and endorsement sends a strong message about the value of each to staff and students. Schools that immerse students in the arts will enjoy a variety of benefits: high test scores; increased attendance; high levels of student motivation; less behavioral problems; sense of belonging, identity, and community; and pride.

NEGOTIATING

PREPARE TO SHARE PROFICIENCY TEST DATA AT THE NEXT FEW STAFF MEETINGS!

During their internship, I gave Jeromey and Dustin some challenging assignments. I was purposely testing their knowledge, work ethic, ability to handle pressure, and skills in thinking on their feet. So I challenged both to analyze our data and present ideas for schoolwide improvement during staff meetings. I knew that for them to speak to the staff as administrative interns would immediately cast them in a different light with numerous peers. It would also challenge their self-confidence and poise. They knew that we would reflect afterwards. I waited to hear their mumbling, complaints, or self-doubts—either directly from them, or roundabout from others—but nothing surfaced. They were ready to take the leap.

It was challenging to remain quiet during the meetings and refrain from answering questions when they faltered. When I remained neutral, they developed responses of their own. They grew in confidence at each meeting, passed my tests, and appeared to enjoy the challenges.

When we reflected, not only did we talk about the quality of their material, but their body language, eye contact, voice quality, confidence level, and ability to respond to questions. Without achieving a high level of trust and developing comfort in our threesome, the potential for our mentoring partnership to move forward would be limited.

Mentee Reflection: Dustin

Little did Paul realize that this task he assigned both Jeromey and me was one of the most interesting, yet nerve-wracking, of all our shared learning experiences. I remember when he came to us and said, "I want you to present your ideas to the staff about how to analyze test data and use the findings to improve student achievement." Neither Jeromey nor I had addressed the staff in the role of an administrative intern. Needless to say, we were nervous. How would we be accepted? How would Paul critique our work? We gathered information, completed a staff survey, and finalized a plan. We were ready, or so we thought!

As we began our presentation, we noticed the body language of our peers in a different way than as teachers. Some was good, yet enough was obviously negative to be unnerving and discouraging. But we persevered and gained confidence with each speaking opportunity.

Our presentation became a foundation for what our staff, under Paul's leadership, would continue to focus on throughout the year. The project also proved very helpful in helping us learn to analyze data, clarify information, and confidently speak in front of adult learners in our own schools.

Although we were anxious when Paul "threw" this project at us, we took it and successfully completed the objectives. Later, we realized how he was testing not only our ability to work with the staff but also with him as a protégé.

Lesson Learned

Beginning principals must be knowledgeable about how to use test data to drive instruction and improve student achievement. But knowledge alone won't lead to success unless the principal is secure in the ability to speak with confidence, understand human dynamics, and persevere against all odds.

In the negotiating stage of the mentoring partnership, the mentor and protégé should work out the details of testing each other, establish comfort levels when addressing personal habits, reflect on what each wants and needs in the role of mentor and protégé, and develop a trusting level of communication.

ARE YOU EVER SURPRISED BY THINGS?

At one of our mentoring breakfasts, I asked both Jeromey and Dustin if they were ever caught off guard or surprised by something in their planning for the day or week. It didn't take long for both to begin sharing experiences. I purposely asked questions of both that I hoped would guide them to create a vision for their schools.

I knew they had struggled with organizing and seeing the big picture, and I hoped they'd be honest about what they'd experienced. And, of course, they were. Here is what we learned.

Scheduling can overwhelm an experienced principal. Not being on top of things can spell disaster for a beginning principal. It is embarrassing to miss an appointment or to be unprepared because of your own inability to sort things out and anticipate events. Early on, I made it a point with both Jeromey and Dustin that I expected them to share copies of their weekly staff bulletins. The purpose of these staff bulletins is to provide a schedule of events for the staff: meetings, assemblies, inservice opportunities, parent activities, important commitments and schedule of the principal, and so on. It also is a vehicle for the principal to describe new initiatives, set expectations, clarify practices, and to do so for all staff in a documented manner. It has always been my expectation that bulletins be read each week. I often find copies in staff planbooks and on teachers' desks.

Both Jeromey and Dustin had read many of mine when they were teachers. Even though both produced nice looking documents with desktop publishing programs, the content appeared vague. Information their staff should know weeks in advance was missing.

I used upcoming collaborative staff development training between our schools as the focal point of the learning opportunity. I questioned how much they thought a typical staff member in either school could tell anyone else about what they were to be learning and sharing when the consultants visited. Were they sure each staff member was clear as to the intended outcomes of this collaboration? Were staff members aware of the grant support we had received? They told me what they had shared in staff meetings, but I inquired about those, like me, who might have missed their meetings. How would they know expectations? Had all details been shared?

As we talked and shared together, I explained how even though the events and activities of the inservice days might be clear in their minds, they had the obligation to enable all staff members to know their expectations and all details of planning in advance of the inservice days. Like with students, if they didn't provide the details and set clear expectations, they couldn't expect students to learn and perform well. I critiqued and told both that from reviewing their staff bulletins, the information was too vague and not timely enough. They needed to plan in more detail and think through all the angles.

Time will tell if the lesson I was attempting to teach was learned. But the practice of sharing bulletins is helpful. We learn from each other. I demonstrate to my protégés how to conceptualize and plan for important events; they teach me new computer tricks and how to remain current with Internet and Web site information. Two and three heads are better than one!

Lesson Learned

Planning and keeping ahead of events is one of the most challenging objectives for the beginning principal. Mentors must observe and find multiple ways to assist their mentee's learning of organizational skills and management of day-to-day and long-range activities.

Without a solid organizational base, it is difficult for one to focus on vision. And visioning is one of the most challenging lessons for a mentor to convey to the protégé.

I'VE HAD IT!

My phone rang just after 5:00 p.m. on a cool, sunny, late March afternoon. I had just put on my running shorts, one shoe, and was tying up the laces. It was Jeromey calling. He started reviewing some business details of a plan to implement a collaborative grant that both our schools had received for special education. Before he could get too far, frustrated with him over what I perceived to be his inaction on various details, I started in on him.

Earlier in the afternoon, I had happened upon what appeared to be a scheduling conflict between several district personnel and the consultant we had hired for the grant. This frustrated me because several times during the school year I had told Jeromey that I hadn't received his staff bulletins via interoffice mail, a common practice in the district. Despite several attempts to get his attention and convey my disappointment, I continued to receive nothing. Had I received his latest, I might have seen that the mistake originated from the other school. I assumed he had overlooked what I perceived to be a major conflict. This time, I let him know I was frustrated and upset. I accused him of failing to follow through with my requests to receive information from his school. I was clear, very direct, and relentless with my chastisement until I heard nothing in response. Suddenly, I realized the reason he had called was to share his experiences of an awful day.

I quickly tried to turn the conversation when I heard him say, "I've had it!" He began recounting pieces of an evolving situation related to the handicapping identification process of a student and his frustration with several staff members. Things had reached the boiling point, and I could sense he needed a friendly ear. I apologized for adding my frustrations to his load. He is always forgiving, and we decided to meet in fifteen minutes for a Coke at Wendy's and a mentoring session.

En route, I mentally reviewed everything I had learned about being a good mentor. I knew I should listen, avoid judgment, and direct his thinking and actions toward positive solutions. I knew it would be hard to remain neutral when the players in the scenario were people I knew.

I hope my advice was beneficial. I missed a good afternoon run, but it was more important to be there for my protégé at that moment than to try to schedule a time to talk sometime in the future. Jeromey made the right decision to call his mentor, described his frustrations, opened up, admitted he didn't know what to do, asked for help, and laid himself vulnerable to what I might say when he needed it the most. The learning opportunity couldn't have been better.

As I listened, Jeromey shared frustrations about

- Shouldering the responsibility and time required for special education decisions;
- The support he perceived from the district office and his authority making student placement decisions involving other schools;
- Insecure adults who cry about their problems in his office;
- A meeting that had been held, without his knowledge, after the supervisor had been called away and during which an IEP was written for a non-qualifying student;
- The reaction when he refused to sign the IEP;
- A multitude of activities, responsibilities, and surprises throughout the day related to a schoolwide hands-on science assembly.

He poured out the details of events leading to his boiling point. I remembered many similar frustrating days.

I asked him what he wanted to experience differently. He knew he had limited knowledge about special education laws, IEP development, and the experience of his veteran staff. But he said he learned each time he participated in a meeting. As he would talk, I tried to help him reflect, focus, and redirect when necessary. I tried to help him see issues from the other people's perspective. The more he talked, the more he opened up. I had never seen him so frustrated or stressed.

We drank several Cokes while I listened, guided, consoled, and helped formulate a plan for the next day. Before he left, he told me that he would meet with his special education supervisor and work to develop trust and a mutual plan for shouldering the responsibilities of the school. He also contemplated how he would address his concerns with his staff and help them better understand his level of expectation regarding their professional behavior and communication. Although no plans were certain, talking relieved his stress. When he left, rather than being defensive and critical of others, he was developing an offensive plan that would lead to clarifying issues and teaching his staff, thus avoiding future frustrating days.

The next morning, I sent the following e-mail to Jeromey:

Remember as a teacher when your kids were "crazy," doing things that drove you mad, acting in ways you knew they shouldn't? Remember what you did to straighten things out? I hope you calmly TOLD them and TAUGHT them what you wanted them to know and to be able to do. It's the same, in many respects, as what you are struggling with and must do to redirect those who work for you now. I'm sure that after a night's thinking, you've got some plans of action in your head. Lead. You're the boss. You'll do it, and you'll feel better after you've talked through things with all the players. Make sure people know how you feel and why.

You were so smart to call. Sorry I dumped on you first.

Call me if things don't get better. Have a great day!

Mentee Reflections: Jeromey

I was expecting the day to be busy because of many planned meetings, yet I hoped it would be normal. It was a Wednesday and that meant many special education meetings. I made sure there was adequate substitute coverage for the teachers involved in the meetings. We also had COSI-on-Wheels, an all day, hands-on science program that involved nearly 70 volunteers as well as every student and teacher. The day before had been very hectic. I had experienced many interruptions due to calls from parents, issues with staff, and the occasional behavior problems from students. To put it plainly, I was up to my ears in work.

The early morning intervention meetings took place as planned, and my morning announcements passed without a hitch. All was calm at 9:10 a.m. I had planned my day so that I could open the COSI assembly and follow that with periodic stops and checks on volunteers. I also hoped to enjoy time with the students. The substitute teachers had been assigned to cover teachers involved in the special education meetings. I also planned to drop in on the meetings from time to time to provide assistance and answer questions. But by 9:30 a.m. my special education supervisor called to say that she couldn't facilitate the afternoon meetings. Then another call came requesting my attendance at an emergency principals' meeting to review our district's emergency plans in view of the impending invasion of Iraq. In the back of my mind my frustration grew as I thought about the work that was piled up from the day before. As the day began to unfold, I soon realized that my plans had to be quickly adjusted.

I focused on the work to be done and tried to multi-task when possible. I tapped any resources I could to help meet commitments as I moved to each event. When I left the building for the principals' meeting, I was sure that all hell would break loose and COSI would be spoiled for the students.

Moving task by task, I was able to make it through the day. I was glad to see the dismissal of the students that day. After the students and most of the staff were gone, I sat in my office contemplating what had transpired. But then I discovered my biggest challenge when I noticed an IEP had been left for me to sign for a student who clearly did not qualify for special services. Problems had been brewing for weeks, and this appeared to be the clincher.

Trying to relax and assess the situation, at about 5:00 p.m. I decided to call my mentor to vent. To my surprise he immediately began venting about some documents he hadn't received from me. That was all I needed. I wanted to crawl under a rock for a month or two. Within a few minutes, Paul realized I wasn't responding, and he asked me to explain why I called. As he listened, he quickly changed his tune and he insisted we meet for a Coke to talk further.

That time we shared was probably one of the most important mentoring sessions we'd ever had. He was very forward sharing his similar experiences. He shared that he'd survived many days like I had just experienced. He guided me to reflect on what I should be doing in the building and how my time needed to be spent. He asked many questions, made me think and talk, and gave me great ideas. After more than an hour, I felt better. I had a plan in my mind of what I needed to do and how I would go about working with my staff to better explain my expectations.

Paul left an important message ringing in my ears that evening. He said it several times. "You're the leader, JUST LEAD!" He helped me focus. I began to understand that the events of the day got out of control because people didn't know what I expected of them. They needed to hear from me. I had to learn to lead. I had to experience this day to know how to make things better. I know I am a better leader for having talked this through with him.

My Action Plan

The next day I called up key people who could teach and guide me in steps that needed to be taken. With the facts I needed in front of me, I called a meeting with the teachers who were involved in writing the IEP and reviewed what happened and how I expected future IEPs to be developed. When the meeting was over, there were clear expectations set for dealing with IEPs in the future and no rocks unturned.

I later met with the special education supervisor and discussed our relationship and where we needed to be headed as a team. We needed to be able to trust each other and make decisions that we could both live with.

There needed to be an understanding with everyone that on days when there were important projects in the building, I might not be available to cover for others' absentmindedness. My priorities and activities for that unfortunate day were changed because the appropriate people could not be at the meeting. The need to cover others' responsibilities pulled me away from where I needed to be, particularly the COSI presentation. Not only was this a lesson for me to learn but one that I needed to share with staff members.

Lesson Learned

The mentor must avoid bringing criticisms, discomforts, disconnects, or feelings that might negatively impact the mentee's willingness to share information and seek assistance in time of need.

Mentors must openly encourage the mentee to initiate frequent contacts in order to avoid unnecessary frustration and worry about their experiences. They must recognize the mentee's anxieties and be available in times of need. They must reassure the mentee that it is good to vent. They should initiate contact with the mentee and model how to vent and share experiences.

Mentors must avoid the trap of telling mentees what to do or how to do it. Learning is more meaningful and valuable when the mentor guides the mentee through a series of possible scenarios and solutions, enabling him or her to think and formulate his or her own plan of action. Time and patience are important virtues.

The underlying lesson of this story is learning the importance of setting high expectations for the performance of adults—creating a vision. When the principal lacks a clear vision and expectations, staff will falter. Clarify what and how you expect things to be done, then hold adults accountable. You can't lead without telling others where the group is going.

LOOK THEM IN THE EYE!

Dustin and I were participants at a meeting in his office. When I was not part of the conversation, I focused on observing my protégé's eye contact while he was intensely involved in thought and dialogue. Ever since he was a student in my college music class, I had privately suggested that Dustin work to improve his ability to make good eye contact with people when speaking. I suspected some vision problems because of glasses, and later contact lenses. And even while he was a teacher, I mentioned some concerns. This particular conference allowed me more time to observe than speak, and I noticed that under pressure, Dustin frequently looked downward for his thoughts before connecting with the eyes of the other person. The things he said didn't cause my sensors to react, but what I didn't see with my eyes did. But I decided that I'd wait for a more opportune time to reflect with him about my concern.

That time came after the other conference participant questioned me about his inability to maintain eye contact, knowing my close relationship with Dustin. He, too, thought Dustin was extremely intense and focused, perhaps struggling and insecure about what to say as well as how he looked while speaking. He specifically mentioned a concern about eye contact. And I knew then that I must meet with Dustin and reflect.

Knowing that another very important person had raised the issue, Dustin listened intently and assured me that he would try harder to eradicate this problem. He accepted my comments and my offer to help. Together we continue reflecting and growing. He doesn't get defensive. And someday, if not already, he'll be thankful a critical friend brought this to his attention.

We've been participants in many conferences and meetings. We watch and observe others. We critique each other's actions, mannerisms, speaking, and leadership styles. We strive to identify situations where eye contact is most crucial. When we talk we make sure both of us look each other straight in the eye. We have contests to see who can stare the other down. We've made this into a game and personal challenge. The outcome will be positive and beneficial for a young principal's confidence and success.

Mentee Reflection: Dustin

I've always thought I had pretty good eye contact, but how do I know? Paul pointed this out to me when I was an undergraduate in his music class. I'll always remember what he said to me then: "Look people in the eyes. You have a lot of potential—you just need to come across stronger when speaking to others." I have always tried to work on this, and as a principal, it is more important than ever. I've always had a strong personality, but improving my eye contact could make it even stronger. Paul has begun to help me with this, and I have greatly improved in this area already. My problem now is that I don't want to glare at people like Clint Eastwood, but I want to keep their attention and let them know that I am following them. I guess I like the idea of being able to stare someone down if need be. It's a sign of weakness if you can't maintain eye contact. I recognize this, and I am doing all that I can to build and improve upon it.

Lesson Learned

Eye contact is important in interpersonal communications. Inability to make eye contact because of habit, lack of consideration, preoccupation with thoughts, or intimidation can cause listeners to question one's confidence, sincerity, and/or ability to communicate effectively. Every protégé should insist that the mentor observe, reflect, and critique his or her eye contact in a variety of conversations.

Strong mentoring partnerships will allow participants to learn together, set goals, and focus on many topics, some of a very personal nature. The effective mentor must not ignore discussions of any issue that could diminish the protégé's potential effectiveness.

NEVER LET THEM SEE YOU SWEAT!

Like the commercial says, principals can't let others see them sweat. It shows one's vulnerabilities and allows others to position themselves in ways that weaken the principal's decisions and authority. Besides sweating, there are other noticeable nervous habits that people exhibit when under pressure.

For the first couple of years that Jeromey worked with me as a teacher, he never failed to present himself to me in polite, respectful, and professional ways. It took months for me to convince him that he could call me Paul, rather than Dr. Young. I know I intimidated him on numerous occasions, always situations where he lacked experience and comfort. When I'd put him on the spot and ask him tough questions, especially in front of others, he'd get flushed and clear his throat before speaking. Most always, what he had to say was on target. But the usual cough or throat clearing I heard before he spoke was a fanfare that he was nervous, intimidated, and unsure.

Now, as colleagues, we have frequent meetings where we observe each other under pressure or in the line of fire of direct questions from superiors or colleagues. Administrators have to make many difficult decisions, and during those times, meetings can become ugly. Tough principals maintain their composure and focus while others allow people to get what they want. There is no allowance for inexperience when the stakes are high and decisions are made that can have lasting impact upon one's school. Beginning principals must quickly jump into the fray, look out for their interests, and speak and communicate in ways that always present an image of awareness and confidence.

Jeromey and I share a relationship in which we correct each other's annoying habits and push each other to excel. I'm sure my comments and our reflection will cause him to listen to himself and change. I just don't want to see him get trampled by others before the lesson is mastered.

Lesson Learned

Mentees will benefit from a mentor or critical friend who will observe and point out aspects of one's public presence that can detract from interpersonal communication. In a close partnership, critiques are mutually accepted without resentment. Where there is a desire to learn, the immediacy of reflection is key to successful adult learning. Together, friends push each other to learn and be the best they can be in all situations.

THE LITTLE THINGS MAKE A BIG DIFFERENCE

I'm as frustrated with myself as I am with my protégés. A consultant had been hired for the week to work with both our staffs. Months earlier, Jeromey and I received a $50,000 grant from the Ohio Department of Education designed to enable our staffs to collaborate for the improved delivery of services to students, particularly those in special education. Now was the time to realize the immensity of what we planned and wrote in the grant, and to do all the necessary work. The grant's intended outcomes centered on improving staff effectiveness in helping all students access and become successful with the regular curriculum and high stakes tests. The responsibilities for implementing the grant were to be shared by all three of us, but with frontline communications left with Dustin and Jeromey as principals of both schools.

I'm frustrated because even after talking about my concerns at a mentoring breakfast, I continued to observe too many little details slipping past my protégés. I purposefully left some of the details to them, such as scheduling, acquiring substitutes and work areas, communication of expectations to staff, and dealing with last minute changes. I sensed that they hadn't listened to or understood what had been discussed in a previous mentoring breakfast. I determined that it was time for them to experience what it's like to drop the ball. They did. They failed some of my tests. They know I am upset and disappointed in their performance. That creates another set of problems that is testing the strength of our interpersonal relationships. We have much we are working through, particularly our emotions and damaged pride. I'm glad they agree to continue to participate in mentoring breakfasts, as we'll soon have a chance to vent, listen, share, reflect, and learn together.

As much as I'm frustrated with each of them for dropping balls, I'm just as angry with myself. I'm struggling with my inability to effectively reflect and sort through three nagging thoughts related to my frustrations. First, I know it is inappropriate to be angry, particularly to let my anger show the way I do, especially if I have failed to effectively set expectations and teach the importance of those things that I expected them to know. Second, perhaps the issue is not my teaching and their learning, but rather their unawareness, lack of intuition, inability to anticipate and see the bigger picture, and inattention to obvious details and common courtesies working with and leading others. Third, if the second issue identifies the reasons they were caught off guard and dropped the ball, then I am extremely frustrated with my inability to visualize what I need to do to teach and help them learn. I can't be a quality mentor to them if I can't figure it out.

What are some of the little things that make a big difference?

- Knowing to initiate final communication with the consultant prior to her travel to Lancaster to review expectations, lodging details, where to report Monday morning; review the schedule; and ask questions.
- Planning and communication among the collaborating principals to "cover all the bases."
- Detailed principal-to-teacher communication, planning days in advance, anticipating glitches, explaining homework expectations, schedules, letting people know where to report, what to take, and reiterating goals and intended outcomes from the inservice.

- Determining a plan for meeting the consultant at the meeting site, assisting with setting up the room, requesting substitutes, arranging for last minute changes, copying handouts, making coffee, providing refreshments.
- Being the first at the workshop site to greet the consultant and the last to leave.
- Arranging the workshop room in the central office in the condition it was found.
- Communicating with each other, communicating with teachers, sharing, brainstorming expectations, listening, learning, and leading.

It is my hope that by focusing on each of our dropped balls we will all learn and improve in the future. My choice to allow the little things to go undone might have backfired. Only time will tell if I can determine how to better teach this lesson—and if my protégés are determined to learn.

Mentee Reflections: Jeromey

In February, Paul and I applied for and won a grant from the Ohio Department of Education. Our schools shared $50,000, enabling us to hire first-class consultants to show our staffs how to incorporate best practices in the area of special education. Obtaining this grant gave us the opportunity to support an initiative that would better equip our staff to meet the needs of students, as required by state and federal standards. Dustin, being the interim principal of West School, also shared responsibilities for the grant implementation.

Paul has had a lot of experience dealing with grants and consultants, but I was unaware of the little details necessary for successfully hosting a productive professional development experience. I thought I had done the preliminary work; I had informed my staff, told them about the grant, secured a large room in our central office for the consultant and staff to work, and outlined what the consultants would be doing. I was ready to offer my staff a solid staff development opportunity . . . or was I?

In May, as the first day of the inservice unfolded, I realized how many of the little details hadn't been contemplated or covered. How did I learn? From my obviously disappointed and angry mentor. He clearly let me know

- That a courtesy call to the consultant to review schedules and objectives was an expectation I'd overlooked,
- That I hadn't arrived at the training site early enough,
- I hadn't adequately prepared the room,
- I hadn't considered making coffee or providing refreshments,
- That he didn't think I had planned enough in detail,
- That I hadn't thought through the small details.

He was not happy! And I realized that his fuse was lit because I had forgotten over and over again to share my weekly staff bulletins with him. I was at a loss for words while listening to him express his displeasure and disappointment.

As this week unfolded, I realized I made several other mistakes.

- I pouted and didn't talk to Paul
- I got angry and didn't focus on what he was trying to teach me
- I let problems fester too long with my mentor
- I forgot still to send him a staff bulletin
- I didn't adequately express my feelings
- I failed to clearly communicate expectations to my staff

By midweek, Paul insisted we meet and clear the air. He came to my office after school. This situation had escalated to the point where both of us were experiencing difficulty sleeping. Stress was affecting my work. I was relieved to talk things through. I probably should have opened up even more than I did.

Once Paul and I worked through our tense moments, we reflected on the lessons learned. I am looking forward to September so I can do better with our next round of professional development. In fact, this lesson was so important that I am already thinking of ways to make our next inservice better.

I've learned that you need to think ahead and have things prepared so that the little details don't sneak up on you.

My advice to other protégés:

- Do not put off initiating a conversation with the mentor when you know the relationship has been strained
- Think more than I did in planning for important events
- Learn this lesson, and pass the tests from your mentor—it's better to be yelled at by him or her than by your boss

---

Mentee Reflections: Dustin

Paul called me early on a Monday morning and I knew he was very frustrated. He has never really "reamed" me out, but he was letting me have it in a nice way during this conversation. I knew that Jeromey and I had slacked off on this workshop. I don't know if it was because of a lack of communication, we forgot, or we just thought Paul was going to handle things as he usually did.

Anyway, we really came across unprepared, and I was actually quite embarrassed. Paul began the conversation by telling me that Jeromey should have been better prepared in informing his teachers, but he quickly let me know that there were some concerns he had with me as well. I think Paul took it hard that he hadn't prepared us for taking care of a workshop like this; however, it wasn't his fault. Jeromey and I had not experienced responsibility for something like this, yet we had watched Paul do it many times as we worked under him as teachers.

After I got off the phone, I called Jeromey and asked him if Paul gave it to him for our mutual lack of preparation. Jeromey explained that Paul had talked to him as well. It hadn't gone well with him, either. We began identifying and dividing responsibilities for the rest of the week to make up for "dropping the ball." Jeromey prepared the room and supplied coffee and donuts the next day, and I did likewise on the following days.

When I reflect on this week, I'm actually glad it happened. Sometimes there is no better way to grow than to learn from your mistakes. As I have mentioned earlier, I do well with constructive criticism. I appreciate having a mentor like Paul. The best way for me to improve is for someone to "tell me like it is"!

Lesson Learned

Teaching someone to be at the top of their game is hard work. To get there, one must attain a vision, see beyond the obvious, and anticipate what must be done at present as well as the future. A principal without vision cannot lead.

The little things make a big difference. Those little details, left undone, can lead to bigger problems. Sometimes, to best teach a lesson the mentor must step aside and allow the mentee to fail and learn from experience. Together afterwards, deep reflection can turn an unpleasant situation into a memorable learning experience.

Mentors and mentees must never permit frustration, hurt feelings, improper behavior, inaction, or lack of communication to strain their relationship. One must initiate contact when a problem arises. Both must be willing to listen and work through the differences. Relationships built on trust and mutual respect will withstand these bumps along the way.

Always be on top of your 'game.' If you're not, someone will notice and it can weaken your credibility.

—Dustin D. Knight

Always plan ahead to stay ahead.

—Jeromey M. Sheets

WHERE ARE YOU?

It was Friday afternoon, and Jeromey and I had planned to meet to review a draft manuscript of this book, discuss timelines, and assign additional writing responsibilities. We planned to meet at a local restaurant at 4:30 p.m. As

I was preparing to leave my school, I became engaged in an important planning and brainstorming conversation with a valued parent. But there was no good excuse for being late for our scheduled work session. I was still driving across town at 4:33 p.m. when my cell phone rang. "Where are you?" he started before blasting into me for my tardiness!

I've always stressed punctuality with my protégés. I don't hesitate to let them know my frustrations if they are late or miss our mentoring breakfasts or sessions. So I knew immediately to expect the same from Jeromey when I realized he was already at our meeting site.

I loved it! My cell phone exploded as he proceeded to "give it to me" in the manner he knew too well from being on the receiving end from me.

I knew he'd learned the value of the punctuality lesson. I loved that our roles had reversed and he was dishing out a little of what I deserved.

Mentee Reflections: Jeromey

It's always interesting listening to teachers and administrators in our district talking about "when I was your age." At first I was a little bothered by this comment and felt a little threatened. Because of my young appearance and my birth date, I felt a little singled out. I am the youngest person in the building and almost always the youngest person at any district administrative meetings. You might say I'm the new kid on the block, and some refer to me as the "pup."

I've learned to deal with the fact that at least for now, I am the youngest principal in the district. Despite my age, I have a job to do. I accept the responsibility to be the best leader that I can be. History shows that Alexander the Great could have been, like me, called a pup, but he ruled very well during his 20s.

Fortunately, I've had the opportunity to work with Dustin Knight. With only a year separating us, it has been nice to know that we both share the same concerns and now hardly realize our age. Together, I know that we can and will grow to be great team and leaders in our district and profession.

Lesson Learned

If you have high expectations about punctuality and chastise your mentee when late, expect him or her to return the admonishment when you are running behind. There was no forgiveness for a three-minute tardiness.

Have a sense of humor and enjoy the moments when you realize your mentor's influence is taking affect.

ENABLING

LISTENING AND THE PRINCIPAL'S RACING MIND

One afternoon I listened to Jeromey describe the whirlwind of events of that day; he could have been recounting many of my experiences as well. I became intrigued by what he described, especially as he talked about the challenges of maintaining focus while listening to people drone and ramble while sharing their multitude of problems. Because he is more laid back and people oriented than me, I never thought I'd hear him describe such frustrations. But like me, he was torn between getting his work done and listening to people go on and on about problems, most of which to him seemed insignificant. His stress was visibly high, he needed to talk, and he wisely sought a critical friend to listen.

Some principals are great listeners. They make people feel special; they connect, and appear capable of devoting whatever time it takes to hear a person out. But I suspect the majority of principals, especially those in large schools lacking adequate support, find themselves experiencing the same dilemma that Jeromey and I and many others know well. There is no debate that successful principals are good listeners. Principals recognize that people will always have issues to discuss, making talking and listening two of the most important daily skills.

But too many good principals share Jeromey's dilemma. They have too much daily work, rarely have two or three uninterrupted minutes, and interact with far too many professionals who can't get to the point. Listening to such people is difficult, especially for highly motivated, energetic, aggressive, bright people. But it can be learned, practiced, and continuously improved. Principals must know how to listen to others' eyes, hands, smiles, frowns, and body language. They must learn to hear what isn't said as much as what is.

As we talked that afternoon, Jeromey shared that he

- Frequently caught himself "zoning out" while listening to some people drone on and on, thinking about the piles of work that needed his attention;

- Dreaded phone calls from frequent-caller, high maintenance parents who could never be satisfied;
- Avoided those staff members who couldn't get to the point in conversations;
- Was amazed by the insecurities and pettiness of certain staff members;
- Recognized that people brought their "monkeys on their backs" (problems) for him to solve, consuming his time, and he saw the need to redirect, empower, and expedite communication.

After trying to console him and help him recognize his feelings to be true and honest, I thought about how a principal could best lead a staff and help improve the daily business of talking and listening for everyone. Even though the principal must have highly tuned speaking and listening skills, what about all the rest of the people who work in a school? We want children to learn these skills, but do the adults model them? Isn't this more than the principal's dilemma?

My hypothesis is that frustrated principals fail to recognize that ineffective talking and listening among all the adults in a school is the root of most problems. They miss the cues that identify adult learners' needs. They allow ineffective talking and listening to derail a sense of structure to their day. If they do recognize the problem, or if they fail to do anything about it, people can monopolize time, say the same things over and over, grandstand, complain, require inordinate attention, and keep doing so day after day. Stress increases as principals have more demands, continuous daily interactions, and interruptions than any other administrator.

Mentors can suggest that mentee principals who relate to this dilemma open themselves to their staffs and share their concerns. If needed, suggest that they seek the assistance of an expert facilitator or consultant. Brainstorm all the problems (experienced by all the adults), and as a group develop norms and a common understanding of how communication can be improved within the school. It's good practice for all staffs to continuously improve their interpersonal communication skills. They can be trained to talk so they get to the point, practice listening, read cues, and become considerate and sensitive of others' precious time.

Students will reflect what is learned and modeled, and everyone will experience less stress.

Mentee Reflections: Jeromey

During my years teaching for Paul, I would observe how busy he was. Many times he would walk down the hallways and not even realize that there were people who had questions, needed to talk, or that students needed attention. It was like his mind was in a different place. In his office, other teachers and I would try to talk with him, but he would keep on writing, typing, or continue to read.

I often wondered why Paul hadn't taken time to stop what he was doing and listen to other people and even me. Was it that he didn't care about the situation or about the staff? I couldn't really understand or explain why sometimes he would get into a zone where he was so focused that everything else seemed to be blocked out. Even during meetings he would move around a lot, look at his watch and sometimes his appearance would show that he had something else on his mind.

It didn't take long for me to experience the same situations and realize that Paul was not doing this to be rude or disrespectful; rather, about half the time he probably didn't realize he was doing it at all. I often find my mind wandering and thinking of more pressing issues as people talk to me about the problems they have. Many times, as I work in my office on the computer, I make it a point to turn and look at a teacher when they talk, no matter how busy I am or what the topic of discussion might be. Remembering the experience of observing my mentor when he was busy, I try to be a more empathetic listener.

To this day I am still working on being a good listener and find it very hard at times. Sometimes I just want to say, "Can't you see that I'm busy?" or "Come back in an hour and my work will be complete and I will give you my full attention." Although this is sometimes how I feel, I know that when a teacher needs to talk to me, I should consider it important and give him or her my time, attention, and advice.

Lesson Learned

Listening is a critical skill for principals. It is absolutely necessary for effective mentoring and leading. Those who listen best are most capable of recognizing the needs of adult learners.

The manner in which a principal listens is perhaps more important than how he or she speaks. People will be more critical of principals they perceive to lack proper listening skills than they will poor speaking ability. Stop what you are doing and listen to people when they talk with you. Make good eye contact, listen to what the speaker says, and observe what he or she is not saying. You may be surprised by what you don't hear!

SEPTEMBER 11, 2001

Once I sorted through all my emotions, informed my staff of the horrific events of the day, and decided to personally inform and reassure my students, I found a few moments to touch base with those closest to my heart. I thought of Dustin and worried how he might be handling things in his new school. He called me before I was able to reach him. I tried to reassure him, shared what I had done and planned to do the remainder of the day, and directed him to the NAESP Web site for information and resources that would assist him in determining what to say and how to work with the people of his school.

It was how the aftermath of the events of 9-11 would affect Dustin that concerned me most. As the weeks wore on, I noticed he was losing weight, his appearance was drawn, and he was always stressed. He was taking deep breaths. He seemed sad. He did not look well or have his usual spark. I became concerned. To my inquiries, he would always respond, "I'm fine."

Eventually one day I took him aside and got in his face. I told him I wouldn't go away until he leveled with me. I knew he was not well. It was then that he began confiding that the events of 9-11 and fatherhood, compounded with opening a new school, had begun to take a toll. He was anxious that he might be called into military service. He found himself unable to break away from the news bulletins and updates on his TV. He was experiencing grief for the victims and becoming paralyzed in his ability to move forward. He was tired of trying to act brave. He needed someone in whom he could confide his inner thoughts; I was glad to be that person.

How I supported my protégé as he shook off his depression is not important to this story. What really is important is that everyone needs people they can depend on in time of need. I never pretended to be Dustin's shrink. I was simply his friend and colleague. We became closer that day and in the days that followed because he learned he could talk to me about anything, particularly his feelings and frustrations. I think he felt better knowing I was just as anxious about world events as he.

Principals across the country were unsung heroes on 9-11 and the days afterwards. They helped children and adults understand the ramifications of the events. They counseled, reassured, demonstrated tolerance and acceptance, and helped keep this country together. These events were most impressionable and stressful for the rookies.

Mentee Reflection: Dustin

Two weeks after I accepted my first principal's position, the tragic events of September 11 stunned our nation. I didn't know what to think. However, as the principal, I knew I had to be strong and help others deal with their emotions. But I, too, was in shock while assessing the situation.

Just after the first plane hit the World Trade Center, my secretary received a phone call from a parent. We sensed immediately that the nation was under attack. Like many, I hoped the plane had accidentally hit the first building; however, as the events unfolded, it became clear that these were no accidents. My secretary immediately became upset. She was a wonderful secretary and very strong willed, but this shook her up, and I could see it in her eyes. Things seemed to be quickly unraveling. I was as a 27-year-old principal, two weeks into the job, engulfed in tragedy and fear, with the responsibility for 325 children and my staff. How could I protect the children? Were they going to target our school next? What do I do if . . . ?

Listening to the developing events on the radio, I had a strong urge to call Paul and hear what he was doing to handle the situation. When I called him, hearing his voice actually gave me some assurance. I was anxious and scared of what "else" could happen, but after talking to Paul it helped my nerves settle, a little.

Around 10:00 a.m. that morning, parents began coming to school for their children. At first I wasn't sure why, but then I understood. I saw in their eyes the same fear I was feeling. They wanted to protect their children and take them home to safety. What I feared might be many parents retrieving their children was in actuality only 15 or 20. My attempts to calm and reassure the parents did little, if anything. Luckily, the youngest children were oblivious to what was happening, or if they knew, they were too naïve to understand the seriousness of the national crisis.

In my third grade hallway, a teacher was upset because her husband was a pilot for American Airlines. In my fifth grade hallway, there was a student whose father was working at the Pentagon, and in the office my secretary was in tears over the day's events.

What was I going to do? I was too young to remember any conflict except the Gulf War. I was born during the Vietnam War, my grandfather had told me stories about World War II, but I had not experienced fear and terror like this. I was scared. Not scared for my life, but afraid for my family and the school community. Although things appeared to calm down by the end of the day, the fear and the thoughts of the unknown stayed with me for a long time. The next day, I attempted to write an assuring letter to parents, letting them know that all safety precautions were in place at our school.

As I reflect back on this trying day, I often ask, "What could have prepared me better?" The answer is always the same: nothing. Am I better prepared now? Yes. Since this tragic event, many schools have developed terrorist attack plans. Safety precautions have been enhanced in almost every sector of our country.

After September 11, Paul and I reflected about what we did to inform and comfort our school communities during this tragedy. We talked about the "what-ifs" and how specific safety plans should be implemented and rehearsed. We even talked about how important it is to take care of yourself and your family. The memories of this day will be with me forever.

Lesson Learned

The principalship can be a lonely and isolated position. Tragic events happen all the time, and people look to the principal for direction and support. Principals must be courageous people.

Principals also need support. It is essential that all principals have a well-developed network of colleagues and friends that will support them through thick and thin. Alone, one is at risk while searching for answers and understanding. Together, people support each other and learn. Make that call when you need the support of others.

WHAT WOULD HAVE HAPPENED IF I'D DECKED THAT GUY?

As he began telling the story, I could tell he was all fired up. As the story unfolded, my emotions also swelled, as I've "been there and done that" many times. But this was one of Jeromey's first encounters with a bullying, hostile adult.

His school's parent organization was holding a spring carnival on a Friday evening. Jeromey was there to assist. Midway through the evening, a ruckus was reported in the darkness of the playground behind the building. Jeromey went to investigate and found one of his students. He assumed the boy was involved in suspicious activities with others, including some adults. He suspected some illicit drug activity and began questioning the child. The boy pointed out an adult in the darkness who had been bothering him, yelling out, "that's the man!" The adult stranger then came forward and became verbally abusive toward Jeromey once he discovered he was the principal. A quick assessment of the situation led Jeromey to believe that the man had no business at the carnival or on the playground after dark. He asked him to leave school property. But the bully began insisting that he was going inside the building. In response, Jeromey determined that for the safety of everyone inside, he would forbid the man entry.

At the entrance to the school, Jeromey stood his ground despite the man's belligerence. Fortunately, by this time Jeromey's secretary had observed the encounter and called the police, who quickly responded. They eventually got the man to calm down and filed a report.

As Jeromey recounted the events, he described his feelings of anger and defensive positioning. I know he could have defended himself had the man swung at him, but he displayed great restraint. His question to me was, "What would have happened if I had swung at him?"

As mentioned earlier, I've been in similar situations and experienced the emotions and frustrations many times before. Maybe it's a male thing that drives our emotions and instincts to get physically engaged. But we know better, and recognizing that, male principals, as well as females, must be able to use common sense and show restraint. It is always best to call law enforcement before a situation escalates to violence. Even though a principal is threatened and might act in self-defense, the repercussions and portrayal in the media can be nasty. Recognizing when to seek assistance is sometimes hard. Minutes are precious when emotions are running high.

Jeromey also had many sets of eyes watching how he handled this situation. Had he appeared weak, the rumors would have spread. Showing restraint, with obvious strength, he best positioned himself to gain respect from those who value civilized behavior and common sense. The bully displayed inappropriate behavior, and Jeromey, despite the temptations, did not lower himself to his level.

My mentoring advice to Jeromey:

1. Follow up with the police to make sure a proper report was filed and determine whether additional charges need to be filed against the trespasser. Write a certified letter restraining the hostile adult from any future access to the school based on behavior displayed during this encounter and a perceived threat to others. Documentation is important, especially if the adult does act inappropriately again.

2. Follow up with the student(s) to determine exactly what types of activities were taking place in the dark on the playground during the carnival. Issue appropriate discipline if activities were in violation of school conduct codes. Determine whether the adult was conducting any illegal activities with students on school property.

3. Follow up with the parents of the student(s) to determine the level of awareness and supervision they had of their children that evening.

4. Inform the superintendent of all actions.

5. Determine what safety precautions may need to be implemented to avoid problems at future carnivals. This would involve the PTO leadership, custodial, security, and other staff involved with the event.

It's unfortunate that events such as this can ruin what should have been an enjoyable family fun night for everyone. But it is a good learning experience for a young, new principal.

Events such as this can be defining moments and present numerous learning opportunities. Principals must pay their dues, confront the challenges, and follow up with strong, legal actions. Eventually the word will get out that the principal is strong, and respect for authority will be gained. Reflection, in which Jeromey immediately engaged with his mentor, will enable him to grow and improve his planning, supervision of the school during public events, and response during subsequent challenges.

I am proud that he handled the issues professionally and with great resolve.

Mentee Reflection: Jeromey

I'm sure that there are many administrators who have experienced situations in which they felt like physically destroying another person for everyone to see. You listen to a person mouthing off and say to yourself, "Man, I would like to give you a lesson that you'll never forget." You also would like to make a clear enough statement so that everyone around you could see and say, " Boy, I don't want to argue with him."

This was the case with me during a winter carnival. I had over 300 participants in the building and one intoxicated adult waiting to go off outside.

While in my office, a child came in and said that one of the sixth grade students had been threatened outside. He said there was an older gentleman, supposedly a drug dealer in the area, threatening to beat up Cody. Surprised and not sure what to do, but knowing that something had to be done, I marched outside to see what was going on. To my surprise there were students running toward me telling me that Cody was getting in a fight.

I ran to the back of the building where a gentleman about twice my age was approaching. I stopped the man and asked if he was having a problem. He began complaining about the boys using language that was very inappropriate. He told me he was going in the building to find their parents. I noticed while he spoke that his eyes were very bloodshot and that he smelled of alcohol.

At that point, I knew I didn't want him in my building around the rest of the children. I asked him to leave and explained that I would take care of the situation at a later date. He insisted that he go in the building, and I again said no. He said that his children were in the building and that he would be getting them. Having never seen this man, I asked for the children's names. He said it was none of my damn business and began to verbally threaten me. As he was cussing, he continued to walk toward the entrance of the building. As we got closer to the door, I advised him not to come any closer. I was standing between him and the door and finally recognized my secretary at the window. I asked her to call the police, and I waited for them to arrive.

The police finally arrived and the man was asked to leave school grounds. Later that night, after the school was cleared, I thought about the situation and how I felt. In the back of my mind I would've loved to take this guy down and teach him a lesson. But I knew that the self-satisfaction of thrashing this man was not worth losing the respect of those I work with. Sometimes the bigger man just needs to walk away.

Lesson Learned

There will be countless unexpected management situations that will tax a principal's nerves and resolve. Principals must always model appropriate behavior and show restraint. There are also times that will require fast action and a tough response.

Always prepare students and adults in advance for special school functions. Plan ahead. Set expectations and teach students their boundaries. Make sure there is always adequate supervision of the school facility and grounds. Realize that there are times when it is necessary to contact the police for help. Learn from others' experiences. Share and reflect with a mentor.

I Just Found Out That I'm the District Test Coordinator!

Less than a month into my first principalship, I was told I also had the responsibility of being the district's test coordinator. Somehow, this important information wasn't mentioned in the interview. Regardless, I had to do my duty.

First, I called Paul and asked for advice in beginning this task. He advised me to speak with my superintendent and the other principals to learn procedures for ordering test materials for each building. He recommended that I ask lots of questions of administrators, teachers, and support staff, then listen for what had worked and what hadn't in the past. Once I'd gathered information, then he suggested how I might piece together a plan. I went to work!

I visited the Department of Education's Web site and found that I was able to order the necessary tests online. But I still had to determine the proper number and type of tests for each school. I wanted to create a clear set of directions and procedures for the other building principals so they could easily handle, administer, and collect the tests.

Periodically, I contacted Paul. He was able to acquire information from his district that I used to successfully complete and carry out my duties. With his advice, a little research, and hard work, I became more and more confident. I realized the benefit of networking and sharing with colleagues. I was complimented by the other principals for providing clear and detailed instructions.

Mentor Reflection: Paul

Dustin's questions about testing caused me to focus on an area that I consider a personal weakness. I hadn't directly shouldered the responsibilities he was facing, but I did my best to provide sound advice. More than anything, I realized he needed reassurance, and listening as he shared his plans, I could sense what seemed practical and similar to my experiences at my school and guided him to consider what I thought was best practice.

I realized that I was enabling and supporting his daily work. He also shared ideas that I later utilized. This task, like many others focused on instructional leadership, goal setting, and creating a clear vision for student and adult learning, has provided never-ending learning opportunities for mentor and protégé.

Lesson Learned

Beginning principals will learn that not every expectation or assignment is discussed in the interview or listed in a job description. When confronted with a daunting task, call a mentor for support.

Sometimes, the mentor's experience isn't any better than the protégés'. But the effective mentor knows how to listen, guide, ask insightful questions, encourage, and identify shortcuts while directing the protégé's search for information.

It is always much easier to work through a challenge with support than in isolation. The outcome is always better, also.

WHAT DO YOU THINK I SHOULD DO?

I know I'm needed when I hear "What do you think I should do?" from the other end of the phone. I also know the protégés are maturing and becoming confident in their work when they tell me what they've done. Frequently, I find my role is to simply reaffirm or reassure.

I've listened and counseled through calls about whether or not to send a student with a cut lip to the hospital for stitches. I've listened to what has happened when anti-government war posters were found nearby a school in trees. I've heard the protégés vent when they are frustrated with personnel. I've guided them through reports and responses to district administrators' requests for information. I've listened. Mostly, I feel they want an ear, a sense of my experience, and sometimes another perspective to compare with the action they already might have initiated. Listening allows me to learn as well; they are giving me good ideas while requesting advice from me.

Often, the outcome of a conversation ends with "What should we do together?" This is cooperative learning at its best. We are much better as a team than as Lone Rangers.

Mentee Reflections: Jeromey

As Paul writes, it has been a great experience having someone to talk to. Both Dustin and I have learned so much from Paul but also know that we can call on each other. The three of us together have been able to come up with some really good ideas and ways to improve our schools and each other professionally.

We look forward to working together as a team. Our district has nine elementary schools, and we will be responsible for 1/3 of the district's pre-K through sixth-grade students. If we continue to share ideas and support each other, there is no telling what we can accomplish.

Lesson Learned

Mentoring occurs in many ways. Some sessions require the mentor to merely guide. At other times, when mutual experiences do not exist and time is precious, a more direct approach may be beneficial. Still other times, the mentee may require nothing more than information, affirmation, or support. Mentors must recognize the phases of mentoring and take pride in the mentee's growth, progress, and independence.

Sometimes, adult learning can best be achieved with affirmation and reassurance.

When in doubt, pick up the phone and call someone you can trust.

—Jeromey M. Sheets

How Do I Write a Reprimand?

"Can I see you for a few minutes? I want to talk with you about a situation I have going on with a staff member," Jeromey asked during a break at a principals' meeting.

He described an incident that had been developing for more than a week. As he recounted the details of the story, he got my attention when he said the staff member had addressed him very inappropriately in his office in front of others. The staff member accused him of not being supportive and favoring parents. I knew he wanted to confide and vent but also seek my advice about next moves. In the short amount of time we had to share, I gathered that he was dealing with a serious evolving situation with a probable disciplinary consequence for the staff member.

At the next break, he finished the story and asked me for advice. As I asked him to clarify several details and actions taken, I was impressed with what he had already done:

- Written documentation recounting the inappropriate comments made by the staff member, date, time, location, witnesses, and what he had said in response
- E-mail response to the staff member copied to the superintendent
- Follow-up responses and interviews with students and parents with whom the staff member had been having problems

Most of all, I was impressed with his calm demeanor while presenting the sequential details of everything that had happened. I could tell he had been very concerned, frustrated, and embarrassed during the encounter. I believed him when he told me he managed to show restraint, act professionally, and deflect as much of the encounter from other staff members and parents in the office as well.

My suggestions and advice focused on sharing similarities from personal experiences; evaluating his options, next moves, and potential disciplinary actions; whom to notify and seek advice from; and how to avoid getting trapped in the political fallout with the union and central office administration. My experience has been that staff who face potential disciplinary actions often manage to twist events and cast shadows on the principal's actions as well as their own. As we were leaving the principals' meeting, just minutes after I had suggested Jeromey provide the superintendent with a full update, he walked up behind us in the hallway. Without hesitation, Jeromey began to provide that update. As a bystander, I was impressed by the self-confidence he displayed as he talked, answered questions, and listened to advice. Where I likely would have become excited, animated, and relived the emotions of the incident while talking, Jeromey was calm and collected, very focused and fair in his reflections about the staff member. I listened. I was proud of my protégé. I was pleased with the advice and support he received from the superintendent. Particularly, it was good hearing, "no one has a right to speak to you in an inappropriate manner, especially in front of students, staff, and parents. You are the principal of that school, and we will do everything we can to support you so that your leadership and authority is not undermined."

Jeromey and I spent some time afterwards at dinner discussing how to write a reprimand, conduct a discipline conference, and plan next moves. We practiced what to say and reviewed how best to keep documentation. He understood the necessity of his follow-up actions and the serious ramifications of any actions he might or might not take. He listened intently as I reminded him how others would watch from the sidelines—his actions and responses would send strong messages to others.

As I reflected afterwards, I recognized the progress and maturity Jeromey was displaying as a young principal. Additionally, I saw my mentoring role evolving from that of teaching to listening and affirming the actions he already had initiated. I was pleased to observe how confidently Jeromey talked and acted. I questioned whether I could have done so well. I know he appreciated the time I spent listening. I had mixed emotions knowing that as he grew, he needed my direct involvement and assistance less and less. But I was extremely proud of what I had seen and experienced.

Mentee Reflections: Jeromey

What does a first year principal do when he gets complaints from parents about a staff member? What happens when that staff member is allegedly talking about the complaints during class time, causing the students discomfort? When does the principal take action? How do you react and what should you do?

Confused? So was I when I learned that a teacher was saying inappropriate things in the classroom. It appeared to be hearsay at first, but after many hours of listening and investigating, it became clear that I had to take action.

With many things confirmed by students and parents, I had no other choice but to find my own answers. I took the usual steps of talking to people and taking suggestions. My mentor told me what he would do and this seemed to be the same advice I got from others.

I scheduled a meeting and discussed the comments with the teacher. In depth, I explained how I could not support her when inappropriate comments and accusations were being made in front of students. I made it clear that there were to be no more comments made in this manner. The meeting ended, and the results . . . to be continued.

Lesson Learned

Most beginning principal preparation programs contain lessons in handling disciplinary situations. But it will be the mentor who plays a key role, providing critical insights while guiding the protégé's learning when faced with the realities of others' improper actions.

There is never a time when a teacher should be permitted to display inappropriate behavior in a classroom without a consequence. It is also very unprofessional for a teacher to be verbally disrespectful to his or her principal, especially in front of students and other adults. Principals must respond with consequences in accordance with school policy and negotiated agreements.

A mentor's pride swells when he observes the mentee handling tough situations with calm restraint and maturity. Although this situation has the potential for additional episodes, the mentor was able to assist by sharing personal experiences, reflecting, listening, reassuring, and guiding the mentee toward his own plan of action.

THAT'S A TOUGH ONE!

This was one of Dustin's first cases of suspected child abuse. It shook him. He learned how to deal with social service agencies and angry and embarrassed parents. He was warned to be suspicious of adults who might make excuses or cover up other problems by deflecting blame and problems to their children. He learned to stay focused on the needs of children.

Mentee Reflections: Dustin

Halfway into my first year as an administrator, I called Paul to discuss a very difficult situation involving young female students. He was attending a meeting in Florida, but he took time to listen and guide me through what should be done to deal with the evolving problem. Two very young female students had been playing around in the restroom. Unfortunately, the playing around turned into a form of inappropriate sexual contact. I was informed once the students' teacher became aware. I immediately began contemplating how I was going to notify their parents. I'd dealt with sexual abuse situations outside of school, but nothing like this. I was confused, nervous, and unsure how I was going to deal with this one.

I proceeded as follows:

- I called Paul to seek his advice as to what I should do first. He suggested I explain the issue to my superintendent.
- I called my superintendent to explain the situation to her.
- I spoke with the teacher to clarify as many facts as I could.
- I called both parents to explain the situation and what I would do.
- Next, I called the child protection agency right away with my information. They began an investigation.
- I again called Paul to reflect and see what further details he might recommend.

I continued to work on this problem for an entire week. I was able to work with the children's services case worker, the teacher, and parents. I discovered that this was a situation that had begun at home and carried over to school. I became frustrated as the parents became upset with me and made accusations that I wasn't doing enough to resolve the problem. I thought I had followed protocol and covered everything I needed to do; however, without hard evidence of what took place, my investigation stalled. After a couple of weeks, I began to see the perpetrating student act out in inappropriate ways. Inappropriate behaviors occurred on the bus and also in the classroom. This became an ongoing problem that involved hours of investigation, negotiation, public relations, and worry. I learned I couldn't please everyone and tried to stay focused on the welfare and needs of children.

Lesson Learned

The principal must ensure that the school is safe and that procedures are in place to protect students and staff. Quite often, situations occurring off campus find a way of gaining the principal's attention. The effective principal establishes relationships with community agencies that share responsibility for support and school success.

Dealing with suspected child abuse is never easy. Always investigate information, make referrals according to law and district procedures, and keep appropriate people informed. Let the professionals work to determine the extent of the suspected abuse. Be cooperative and protect the welfare and interests of children.

NON-RENEW A TEACHER . . . HOW?

Unfortunately, not all school employees perform in a satisfactory manner. New principals will quickly find themselves facing issues of accountability and evaluative decisions regarding each individual staff member. Effective principals learn to assess strengths and weaknesses and develop strategies that help others reach higher levels of performance. Most often, their efforts as instructional leaders have positive outcomes. But they also must recognize those situations where a staff member's termination is best for children.

Mentors likely have many experiences they can share with their mentee about an ineffective staff member. For the mentee to open and share his or her experience, high levels of mutual trust must exist in the partnership. Not knowing the person being discussed, the mentor must listen carefully, ask thoughtful probing questions, discuss procedural guidelines unique to the district, and caution and advise when appropriate. Most of all, the mentor guides and supports.

Staff terminations are a serious and consuming business. No principal should ever take on such a challenge without the moral support of a trusted mentor and friend.

Mentee Reflections: Dustin

Already, in just two years, there have been numerous situations that have had great impact on my administrative career. This story is one of the most memorable (so far).

In my first year, my first school housed 320 students and 15 teachers. One teacher stood out when I first met her. She was a new first-year teacher hired by my predecessor. As the year progressed, she experienced difficulty performing her duties. Parents were complaining as well as other teachers. "Suzy" was one of two special education teachers. She was responsible for six students.

My first observation of her performance was prearranged. I walked into her small room, sat down, and noticed she was sitting at her desk while several students were working independently or playing around! I kept waiting for her to begin a lesson so that I would have something to observe. I waited and waited. Nothing. For 30 minutes, during a planned observation, she did not teach. To make matters worse, she neglected and mishandled student discipline in my presence.

I walked out of the room thinking, "What was that all about?" I did my best to write up the observation, despite the meager data I was able to collect. As positive as I tried to be, I just couldn't help pointing out concerns about instructional issues. I followed up with a conference and explained that next time I would like to see her "teach."

As the year progressed, Suzy experienced numerous other difficulties. Approximately 70% of the school's discipline problems came from her room. Her performance never seemed to improve, and I was working hard to provide her with support. As the year progressed, I began to realize that I might have to non-renew a teacher. I was communicating with my superintendent, and she was aware of the issues and my concerns. I was appreciative of her understanding and support.

But what helped even more was being able to talk confidentially with Paul. I would often have him review and critique my written observations of Suzy's work. This helped greatly.

In April, I had to review my observations and make contract recommendations at a meeting with the superintendent and board of education. Based on my observations, evaluations, and conversations with my superintendent and Paul, I decided that this teacher was incapable of providing our students with a quality education. I recommended to the board that she be non-renewed, and they supported me unanimously. Although this was a difficult task for a first year principal, it provided me with a valuable learning experience.

You will often hear that it is "lonely at the top" as an administrator. This is so true, but you don't realize it until you're in the position. Talking to my mentor helped me deal with my anxieties and "loneliness at the top."

After this incident, I did grow as a principal. I learned that I must be firm in my decisions. In an attempt to balance negative with positive, I was actually making comments that were contradictory. I didn't want to come across as a "my way or the highway" administrator. From this experience, I learned to become more authoritative.

Paul offered good advice in this situation based on his experience with similar situations. As I watch him, he seems never to "soften the blow," yet I know there is another side. I hope I can become better at being firm and direct, always telling it like it is.

Lesson Learned

Staff evaluations are serious business. Good documentation, clear directions, and recommendations for improvement are essential when evaluating ineffective employees. Be thorough and consistent. Remove those who can't adequately perform.

Just as with writing reprimands, the mentor's experience and guidance can support the protégés' learning, reduce stress, avoid pitfalls, and affirm high expectations for the social and professional development of all staff.

BE CAREFUL WHEN TRYING TO SOFTEN THE BLOW

Dustin called one afternoon after becoming aware that a union representative had been at school checking with a teacher about the issuance of a one-year probationary contract. He described the situation with the teacher and the actions he had taken. The central office staff and board of education had already approved his contract recommendation, yet he questioned whether he had done anything wrong. I wondered why he was calling. Perhaps he knew my history with mediocre teachers and hoped to avoid the wrath of the union, or maybe he was holding back something he hadn't told me. I tried to listen, reassure, and guide until he told me what he had said to the teacher. I quickly saw the need to teach. This is the rest of the story.

While walking down the hallway, Dustin had been questioned by the teacher. In her classroom, she asked about the probationary contract. From her questions and the comments she made, Dustin gathered that she was not fully aware of the serious implications of her performance. I could tell that Dustin had been uncomfortable with the conversation. I vividly remembered how I'd felt in numerous similar situations. He tried to soften the blow by saying, "You don't have any *major* problems, but there are four or five areas in which you will have to demonstrate improvement before I can recommend a contract extension." At that, I immediately interrupted and said, "Dustin, wait a minute! Do you hear the contradiction in what you just said? I know why you might have said it, but the union will challenge you for comments that contradict."

One of the most difficult challenges for any principal, especially those beginning, is documenting and working with ineffective teachers. The tendency is to be humane and give the person the benefit of the doubt. But union representatives will challenge the principal's procedures, comments, and actions as they work to protect the rights of a weak teacher. So once you've determined that the employee manages a classroom where you wouldn't place your own children, or is someone you wouldn't rehire or you wouldn't transfer to your best friend, you have to deliver a strong message in a firm and fair manner. Keep the focus on observable actions and behaviors, and most importantly, what is good for kids.

I think Dustin heard me—loud and clear. Many times while he was an intern, we had reflected on my experiences with weak employees. I had consulted and advised on other situations he'd experienced as a new principal. We continue learning together. Working with mediocre and ineffective employees is always difficult.

Dustin made several wise choices following this encounter in the hallway. He called his mentor. His self-doubts and stress levels hopefully were reduced after talking with a confidant. He reflected and analyzed what he had just experienced. He will have an experience base that will enable him to speak more directly in the future. He learned that others have already walked in his shoes. He openly shared his feelings. He learned and should have "a voice" echoing in his ears the next time he has to deliver a strong message. He learned the dangers of softening the blow. His skin became a little tougher. He grew as a principal.

Lesson Learned

Staff evaluations are an important responsibility for principals. It is the common methodical process principals utilize to establish a vision of effective instruction and expected levels of student achievement.

Even for those principals who interview and hire well, there will be those employees that for some reason just don't work out. Because of the lengthy evaluation procedures detailed in negotiated agreements, appeals, and multi-layered legal rights of teachers, many principals tend to minimize the evaluation process as a way to deal effectively with ineffective performance. Others get caught up in the emotions of destroying another's career. Principals try to soften the blow, and as a result, they get hammered later for poor documentation of inadequate performance.

Learn to be firm, direct, and reflect on observable behavior and performance. Set realistic, measurable goals and timelines. Don't waiver. If the employee can't meet minimal expectations, be courageous and work for dismissal. Keep a focus on the needs of kids. Seek counsel from your mentor.

Having a mentor to help you through your first year can be the difference between night and day.

—Dustin D. Knight

DEALING WITH IRATE PARENTS

It's easy to understand why some people begin looking elsewhere for jobs when they have repeated experiences dealing with irrational people. Unfortunately, in today's society, increasing numbers of people are experiencing deep emotional problems and are unable to cope with their circumstances. They bring their problems to the schoolhouse door. Principals are expected to know how to deal with them and arrange help even when they don't appear to want it. When first confronting these experiences, beginning principals will get the best advice and support from mentors who have extensive experience and have "walked the walk."

Read Ruby Payne's *A Framework for Understanding Poverty*. She provides great insights into the lifestyle and behaviors of people of poverty, middle class, and wealth. Her analyses of the hidden rules and language of those in poverty can help a principal lead a school staff in developing an appreciation and understanding of others. Knowing what to say, how to listen, what to expect, and why to anticipate certain behaviors can help a principal remain calm and collected while remaining focused on issues rather than reacting to emotions.

Mentee Reflections: Dustin

Dealing with difficult parents is never easy. But principals deal with them all the time. As a new principal, dealing with the first angry parent can be a shock. How do you deal with an adult who is irrational? What do you do when they begin yelling in front of their children?

During one particular incident, a parent began yelling at a teacher and me. At first I wasn't sure how to handle what was happening, but I quickly realized that I had to diffuse the situation. My plan of action was spontaneous, but it worked.

- I calmly talked to the parent.
- I then told the parent that I would be happy to talk to him if he would calm down.
- The parent did calm down after he realized I wouldn't interact with him when he raised his voice inappropriately in front of his children.
- I explained the policy of the school so he understood our actions.
- The parent left the school visibly upset, but I followed up by calling him at home.
- Last, I informed the superintendent of what happened, should he get a call from the parent.

Not all irate parents can be dealt with in this simple manner. Some are just plain crazy! I've learned to be flexible and handle situations in different ways. I must remain calm and confident, handling situations as they arise.

Another parent became extremely upset at a parent meeting. She was embarrassing herself and others. I'd dealt with her many times before and knew that she was very unstable. She had been denied access to the school during regular school hours. When she wouldn't calm down, I began to worry and view her as a threat to children and other adults. She was disrupting the meeting.

Things quickly spun out of control. She became extremely irate and disrespectful to me. She even began complaining about her dealings with Paul. I was at a loss as to how to deal with what was suddenly happening. People were watching. Somehow, I remember calling Paul on his cell phone. I knew he was traveling, but I prayed he'd answer. Fortunately, he did. I explained what was happening and asked him what I should do. He advised me to do the following:

- Calmly request that the parent settle down or leave the building.
- Be firm and let her know that if she didn't regain control of herself, the police would be called.
- Follow through and call the authorities to have her escorted from the building if she continued causing a disturbance.
- File a police report and forbid her access to the school at all times.

His focused advice reassured me. He reaffirmed what I knew I needed to do. Fortunately I didn't have to call the police, as she left the school using very foul language with her children in tow.

This was a stressful situation. I did write a letter that officially banned this parent from the building, as she was an obvious threat to the safety and well-being of the children and staff.

Not all situations are this severe, but it is important to have a plan in place and be able to implement it so that an angry parent doesn't become a serious problem. From my experiences, I've learned to

- Stand firm and let the parent know you will not tolerate disrespect;
- Calmly try diffusing the situation by suggesting the other person relax, take a deep breath, take a seat, etc.;
- Reschedule a time to talk if they won't calm down. Should the parent continue to disregard your directions, call the authorities;
- Call my mentor for advice;
- Document what happened, and if necessary, ban threatening people from the school grounds for the welfare of others.

Lesson Learned

Understand that irrational parents are afraid. They lack a mature perspective and experience circumstances in their life unlike anything the principal may know or have experienced. Remain calm, focus on issues, and never allow yourself to treat an irrational person in an inappropriate or disrespectful manner. These can be among the most stressful experiences for principals. How one responds, and there is always an audience watching, has serious ramifications. Remember to call a mentor for support.

A Sexual Predator Where?

West School is located within three blocks of a homeless shelter. Frequently, the wayward men who spend time there cause concern for the local residents. Rumors spread quickly. The staff is constantly alert to suspicious characters, and lessons about strangers are always reinforced with students.

Having experienced situations like this many times, it was interesting to listen to Dustin explain what happened and how he responded to the scenario that follows. Sometimes the mentor's job is to congratulate the mentee on a job well and thoroughly done. This is when the mentee calls you afterwards instead of before taking action, and you feel yourselves bridging to the new relationship of colleagues.

Mentee Reflections: Dustin

It was early in the school year and I was attending a superintendent's meeting with other principals when I received the phone call. A strange man had been seen driving by the playground during recess with his pet dog hanging out of the window. My secretary first informed me of the situation, and I also spoke to the teacher left in charge during my absence. I explained the call and situation to my superintendent, and he immediately gave me advice and suggested what I should do. I returned to school and

- Called the police, explained what had been observed, and requested support;
- Ensured the safety of the students and staff. I had a police officer come to the school as we walked the perimeter of the building;
- Spoke again with the teacher who was left in charge and then wrote a memo to the staff to make them aware of the situation;
- Reviewed a list of sexual predators who lived in the area and made it available to the staff;
- Spoke with the police again and found that they had narrowed it down to two people, had been to their homes and issued warnings;
- Wrote a letter to the parents informing them of the situation and assuring them that all safety precautions were in place. I requested that they be alert and inform me or the police of suspicious strangers in the neighborhood.

This situation potentially could have been very serious, but thanks to collaborative efforts from the community, police, and school system it resolved very well. I learned to

- Be alert to strangers in and around the school;
- Develop a good relationship with local law enforcement;
- Clearly communicate with staff, parents, and the community.

Lesson Learned

Unfortunately, there are sick people in the world. Schools, as public places, from time to time become center stage when dealing with suspicious people and intruders. Principals are naïve to think that "nothing can happen to me" or "bad things won't happen at this school." It is best to err on the side of caution. Develop good relations with law enforcement authorities, rely on their advice, protect the interests of the school community, and communicate openly and clearly when others must be informed.

FREEZING UP THE DISTRICT'S E-MAIL SERVER

I love the fact that Dustin wants to know more about technology than me. Our healthy competition drives us to learn everything we can. We share learning experiences. I'm fascinated by what both Dustin and Jeromey can do with technology and motivated to learn even more. I would be embarrassed to fall behind. From experience, I know the lonely frustrations of not fully understanding how to use a computer program or other technology. One of the most pleasant outcomes of mentoring is finding good instructors that patiently teach me what I need to know.

Mentee Reflections: Dustin

While completing my administrative internship with Paul, I was impressed at how technologically savvy he was. He was always showing Jeromey and me what he was doing with technology and how to do it. As I began my career as a principal, my goal was to be better at technology than Paul!

While serving as interim principal in Paul's school, I think I achieved my goal. I developed a plan to place the school's attendance online, spiced up the school's Web page, enhanced staff bulletins, and implemented other technology initiatives.

The day before Paul left for the NAESP National Conference in Anaheim, he showed me his president's report in the form of a PowerPoint presentation. It was really good. After viewing the presentation, I told Paul that it would be great with some inspirational music. I had had some experience with PowerPoints, so I began to show Paul how we could make this presentation spectacular. Immediately both of us started thinking of special music that would enhance the presentation. We found two uplifting songs that fit very well. We figured out how to add the music and adjust the timing. We were pleased with the outcome.

I was proud that I had shown my mentor how to use a new aspect of technology. I e-mailed the presentation to Paul. I was pleased that I had put music to his presentation and helped him develop it into a "masterpiece." But we suddenly learned, however, that it is not a good idea to e-mail PowerPoint presentations containing over 100 pictures and two full wave songs!

Neither of us could retrieve the PowerPoint via e-mail. Everything froze. We even jammed Jeromey's system at his school. Luckily our district technicians resolved the problem, slapped our wrists, and explained to us why we couldn't e-mail huge PowerPoint presentations. Although Paul's presentation went well without the music, I was still disappointed that what I had taught him he was unable to use.

This was a great learning experience for both of us. I enjoyed sharing with him and being the teacher. I know he enjoyed the role of student and wants to learn more.

Lesson Learned

Mentoring is best when focused on learning. In this case, the mentee clearly possessed the knowledge and became the teacher and guide. The opportunities that mentor and mentee have to learn objectives not necessarily related to their mentoring partnership are special. They help solidify the bond and provide the mentee with a chance to shine.

FOLLOWING IN THE FOOTSTEPS OF AN EXPERIENCED INSTRUCTIONAL LEADER

Prior to my return to West Elementary as interim principal, the school's reading proficiency test results at grades 1, 4, and 6 were the highest in the district. Also, it was just announced by the Ohio Association of Elementary School Administrators that West School was a "Hall of Fame" school. The staff and students were earning a reputation for beating the odds. I had big shoes to fill and felt pressured as an instructional leader to maintain and improve student achievement. How was I going to do this?

First, I began by building upon what had worked in the past. I shared a grade distribution showing all teachers their scores and record of performance over a multi-year period. Then, I broke down the test data to show the teachers what areas needed attention at specific grade levels. I provided teachers with information in the form of student data, graphs, and ideas to improve in specific skills. For example, the students in third grade were struggling in mathematics so we analyzed the data and identified specific skills (measurement, estimation, etc.) in which our students were performing below the basic standard.

After a long, hard year of providing data, analyzing it, and developing differentiated instruction for individual students, we did make improvements. But I couldn't top the previous year's "highest reading scores." However, I learned valuable lessons analyzing Paul's practices and procedures and added some of my own to provide the instructional leadership I felt the staff needed.

Mentor Reflection: Paul

I still get chills when I reflect on the cheer echoing throughout my school that June day when I announced our reading scores. It was the final hour of the last work day for teachers. We didn't have time to celebrate before my departure to serve the next year as President of NAESP. Proud as I was, however, I realized the shadow that would be cast on Dustin when school resumed.

Dustin and I talked frequently about his initiatives. He asked insightful questions. He had good ideas and plans. He refrained from mentioning my name with the staff and avoided conversations that would have reversed direction. Rather than instruction, our mentoring conversations often focused on human interaction issues that developed as he led the staff. It helped him to know I shared many of the same issues. I was pleased that he could relate better than I with some people. Yet with some of the most challenging, like me, he saw a block to gaining higher student achievement.

It was no surprise that the test results regressed toward the mean. But we learned and proved that with hard work, poor kids can learn. With the right people, high expectations, resources, and good old fashioned hard work, we can do it again.

Lesson Learned

Never publicly criticize the work of your predecessor before walking months in his or her shoes. Build upon past practice, identify areas for improvement, use data to support your decisions, and focus always on what is best for children. Learn from your predecessor, build upon success, and realize that the most detailed plans get derailed if the people involved don't share the same vision as the leader.

Instructional leadership is challenging. Much of the challenge of achieving goals is engaging the staff to accept change. The distractions that develop can easily disorient a beginning principal. Stay in close contact with your mentor until you have adequate experience and can successfully establish a vision for all to see.

WHAT IT WAS LIKE TO BE THE INTERIM PRINCIPAL FOR THE PRESIDENT OF NAESP

Mentee Reflection: Dustin

After completing my first year as a principal, I was called to interview for a principal's position in Lancaster, realizing the opening was a one-year interim principalship at West Elementary. Paul was planning to be on leave for a year while he served as President of NAESP. I wasn't really looking for a new job as I was very happy where I was. I was in a medium-size elementary school with approximately 320 students and 15 teachers. I knew if I went to West Elementary the responsibilities would double. But Paul encouraged me to at least go through the interview.

I went through the interviewing process and was offered the job. My only concern was that I was leaving a principalship for a position that had questionable security. Would I have a job after the year? Where would I be placed? Would I be able to try some of my own ideas as an interim principal? How can I possibly succeed by following a nationally known veteran principal? These were just some of the questions that were going through my head.

After a lot of thought and discussion with my wife, I decided that this would be a good move and great opportunity. My previous district had offered to give me an additional four year contract to stay; however, the new position gave me a two year contract, a substantial raise, and it was three miles from my home. The pros outweighed the cons.

I was excited to begin a new school year in the school where I previously taught third grade. I was also a little nervous. With 420 students, 62 special education students, and 55 staff members, I wondered if I would be able to meet all the challenges. Paul had the school running like a "finely oiled machine."

As the year began, I could tell things were going to work well. Paul was a phone call away if I had any questions, and I was now working as a colleague with Jeromey Sheets, my internship partner and former teaching colleague. Although the year started off great, I wasn't prepared for some of the things that happened to me at West Elementary.

First, I had four secretaries over the course of the year! This made office operations extremely difficult. An experienced, capable secretary is crucial to a school's smooth operation. I found myself running both the office and the school. The problems were not due to inability but rather to inconsistency. I had to explain things repeatedly and train each new secretary. This presented an ongoing challenge—and there were others.

Observing and evaluating 55 staff members requires great time management skills. Getting to know the staff and allowing them an opportunity to know me was also a lengthy process. Those who knew me as a colleague and third grade teacher two years before now had to adjust to me as the "interim." This was tough. There were times when I wanted to change or start something new, but I moved cautiously as the interim principal. Deep down, I knew it wasn't *my* school. Since I was filling in for Paul, I focused on maintaining what he had in place, all the while keeping the staff under control so they wouldn't take advantage of me or try to change procedures.

To further add to my challenges, Paul had implemented many programs that needed upkeep and maintenance. In fact, this building had many more activities and programs than most schools (what would you expect from the president of the NAESP?). I found myself consulting frequently with Paul. I was glad that he was available to provide information and guide me as I dealt with numerous situations.

The year was challenging, and at times I wondered why I chose to leave my first school to serve as an interim. But I know the challenges and opportunities that presented themselves in this position helped me learn. Was it worth it? Absolutely.

Lesson Learned

Some people create opportunities for themselves while others watch. Opportunities present themselves in a variety of ways. Don't be afraid to take risks and accept challenges. People never stretch themselves and grow unless they do.

OBSERVING MY MENTOR

Dustin and I have talked numerous times about styles of leadership, the sound of one's voice, presence, and confidence that comes with experience. Knowing that he would serve in my absence for a year, we anticipated many of the comparisons that people would make about us. He readily accepted the challenge to "walk in my shoes." And he did a good job.

Mentees, rather than focusing only on their immediate needs, should always look for ways they can observe and learn from their mentor. They need to add to their personal inventory of skills the things they see that work best for them while always observing and learning from many others. One's style and comfort take years to perfect. Learning occurs each minute and day of those years.

Mentee Reflections: Dustin

Towards the end of the school year, our superintendent allowed me the opportunity to spend time in my new building and work with the principal as a "transition period." He asked me who I would like to substitute for me, and I said, "Well, if you wouldn't mind, Paul Young could cover. That way he can transition back into his building." The superintendent agreed, and a transition plan was put in place.

I was given two days to observe and learn the routines of my new school less than two miles from West School. On the second day, Paul had asked if I would attend a meeting he was going to conduct with his (my) staff. I jumped on the opportunity for a couple of reasons. First, I hoped he would say good things about my work and thank me for serving as interim principal during his year as NAESP President. Second, I wanted to observe him in action as a principal. The last time I had had this opportunity, I was a teacher!

Once he began the meeting, I immediately noticed how quiet the staff became. Paul had their attention, and all eyes were on him. As the meeting continued, I listened closely and observed Paul at work. He had great eye contact, and his statements were clear and direct. I began contemplating how I would manage a staff with his experience. He appeared to make statements and comments with ease, at times delivering news that made some teachers uncomfortable, but he was "telling it like it is." I realized that I have a different communication style than Paul, but I was considering how I might become more direct like him—but in my own way. This was a great learning experience, and I hope to have my style perfected in 24 years!

Lesson Learned

Beginning principals must realize that their mentor can say and do things with what appears to be ease and comfort because of experience. It is wise for the mentee to observe, ask questions, reflect with the mentor, and practice to achieve comfort with leadership styles for various situations. The best protégés have an internal motivation to learn and improve. They initiate conversations and ask for critical feedback. They realize there is no substitute for experience and "paying one's dues."

COLLABORATING

My responsibilities as President of NAESP kept me away from Lancaster and my school most of the year. Listening to me during our breakfast meetings, Dustin and Jeromey gained awareness of the inner working of their professional association, but they missed opportunities to observe me in action as a principal, modeling ways to lead as well as completing the routine tasks of the job. It is with excitement and purpose that I look forward to returning to West School so that I can challenge myself to be their best role model. Each partnership will be different, the relationship between each mentor and protégé unique. Mentoring can be accomplished from a distance or close proximity. But there are times when side-by-side modeling can be a powerful instructional strategy. Don't overlook the importance of those opportunities.

Mentee Reflections: Dustin

As mentioned previously, Paul Young covered for me as I transitioned into my new school. On the second day I returned to West School early to clean off my desk and discover how the day had gone. As soon as I walked into the office, a teacher with two of her unruly students met me. Realizing Paul and I were both in the office, she asked, "Which one of you wants to deal with this one?" I jokingly referred her to Paul but assumed responsibility for the problem. As I did, Paul helped me talk to one boy with whom he was familiar. As we were both talking to this boy, I experienced a couple of interesting feelings. First, I was handling a discipline problem in front of Paul and doing quite well. I was proud of this. Second, he was helping me, and it felt like we were a team. Although it was for a short time, working collaboratively on this problem provided me with insights into how it would be to work together in the same school. As a mentor and mentee, we have shared many events in past tense, but this day, I experienced an authentic "hands on" learning activity.

It's fun and important to learn from your mentor. But as Paul has always said, he has learned as much from working with Jeromey, his other mentees, and me. I hoped what he learned while observing me that day made a positive impression.

Lesson Learned

Learning takes place even when you least suspect it. Adults learn best when they are self-directed and see a specific need to know something. They also have a strong need for immediacy of action. Mentors must understand that they will always be onstage when interacting with their mentees. They must always work to be the very best they can be.

Mentors learn to guide, nurture, advise, listen, question, coach, and teach, often during reflective sessions, during phone calls, through e-mails, and other forms of interaction. Never underestimate the importance of modeling in a mentoring partnership.

WORKING WITH THE MEDIA

Purposefully, I didn't fully inform Dustin about what I suspected might happen. I knew the host of a local cable television show was coming to our afterschool center to do a feature story. I invited Dustin to join me, thinking that we both might be interviewed as part of the talk show. We were. I knew he'd have been nervous if he'd had time to anticipate his first television interview. My setup left him little time to fret. I pushed him in the water and expected him to swim. And he did!

Principals must learn to work effectively with the media. It's common fare to watch television news teams arrive at a school in a time of crisis or when they attempt to break a big story or investigation. And they expect to talk with the principal. The suddenness of the transpiring events can be an intimidating experience. That's why I placed Dustin in the position I did. I knew this interview would be positive and his first experience would be painless.

Preparation and experience help when working with the media. Building positive relationships with publishers, editors, and reporters is also important. Practice. Know the issues, and stick to your points. Identify two or three things you want to say, and stick to them. Say them over and over in your mind and on camera. Think of a sound bite you'll be comfortable hearing on the news and reiterate it. Speak calmly as though conversing with a friend. Look directly into the camera and remain natural. Don't allow clever reporters to twist your comments and lead you into areas you don't want to go. Buy time. Don't respond to reporters' requests until you've had time to prepare. Call a mentor to seek advice if time allows.

The media can be quite helpful in conveying a message, or they can embarrass you. Effective principals understand the importance of preparation and gaining positive experience.

Mentee Reflection: Dustin

He really didn't tell me I was going to be interviewed for a television program. So when I began, I was a little nervous; however, I got over that right away. I actually enjoyed it, relaxed, and let the interviewer run things. I felt comfortable answering questions and tried to talk freely. After my interview, I had the opportunity to watch Paul respond to questions during his time in front of the camera. I could see the experience! He was relaxed and answered each question with ease. He was good with the camera. This was a great learning experience and I look forward to getting more practice.

> ### *Lesson Learned*
>
> Working with the media is an important part of a principal's responsibility. The beginning principal will quickly learn the media's important role in engaging community support for schools.
>
> Become a competent spokesperson for the school. Designate a reliable spokesperson in your absence. Stay on the offensive with the media, and implement the tips for success when encountering tough situations. Contact a mentor for advice. Stay calm and buy time to rehearse the points you desire to make. Pay forward today by building positive relationships with your local media representatives.

CLOSURE

MAYBE WE SHOULD MEET SOMEWHERE ELSE

After more than a year in the enabling phase, it became apparent that my protégés were increasingly secure in their job performance and that our breakfast meetings had evolved into sessions where we planned as collaborators for special projects, as equals. Jeromey appeared to be uncomfortable one morning, speaking with a hushed voice. The typically spirited conversation wasn't occurring, and I sensed that Dustin also was uncharacteristically reserved.

Finally, Jeromey shared a concern that the discussions we were having might be overheard by strangers. He expressed his discomfort with the public setting and suggested we meet in another location. He was fearful that our voices might carry and our actions might be discussed by others. Despite our best intentions, we might not be perceived by others in a positive way.

I realized that we'd all become public figures. Community members recognized each of us as principals and they were discussing our presence together. It was time to reconsider the effectiveness of our meetings, determine continued meetings in public vs. private settings, and begin discussing the closure of some aspects of our mentoring partnership.

I think Jeromey and Dustin would have continued our early Saturday breakfasts had I insisted. But Jeromey's sense of security had been rattled, and it was time to evolve. The enabling gradually slowed as the experience and confidence levels further increased, yet my phone rang when either faced a serious situation. Sometimes, friend to friend, my response was direct, simply to listen, sometimes to offer advice, but more frequently to affirm and commend.

Mentee Reflection: Jeromey

Saturday morning breakfasts were a time to reflect on my development and progress as an instructional leader. I looked forward to talking with my mentor and thoroughly explaining the situations I faced. We would talk about procedures, upcoming events, and necessary preparations. We also sometimes talked about individual staff members, parents, and other colleagues in the district. Management issues almost always included challenges of human resources. To be a leader in an educational environment, I was learning the intricacies of understanding and dealing with people. Paul helped me develop special insights into numerous people who affected and influenced my leadership ability.

As I began my principalship, we met frequently. My mentor's influence and his impact in various educational arenas influenced my leadership development. But as I became more and more confident and further studied the theory of leadership and change, I realized how hard it was to always be compared to my mentor. I realized that every leader had a unique identity, and that I had to establish my own. But I also realized what a wonderful opportunity I had working with a mentor who encouraged me to emulate traits that worked for me and to step out on my own when ready. With Paul's help, I think I've developed my own identity, yet I recognize his influence in much of what I do.

Saturday breakfast meetings gave me a chance to challenge my beliefs, reflect, and solidify my style of leadership. It was great to talk with a veteran administrator, but also a friend. We'd often wonder why people acted and felt the way they did. Together, we would brainstorm strategies to better understand the situations we were experiencing, how to improve communications, and how to lead.

But one morning, as we talked together, I realized what we were saying could be misconstrued by strangers. More and more, the patrons in the restaurant were acquaintances of one or all of us. I questioned our location. We pondered whether it was time to move elsewhere or restructure how we met. People knew we were principals and friends, and they also might like to eavesdrop on our private conversations.

Since then, we've mutually realized that we've come to the final phase of the mentoring partnership. I hope Paul won't ever stop helping and guiding, but the sense of immediate need for his support and guidance seems to decrease with each year of experience. We are friends, confidants, and colleagues. Mentoring has made my development as a principal an exciting learning experience.

> ## *Lesson Learned*
>
> The enabling phase of a mentoring partnership requires the most time, and can last a few months or several years, depending upon the individuals. But there will be an end, obvious or not, and mentor and mentee should prepare for it. The mentor should look for signs and acknowledge an appropriate opportunity for closure before pressures mount and feelings are hurt.
>
> A successful partnership supports a continuance of enabling as needed—even further negotiating of interpersonal relationships—long after the closure phase has passed. Mentor and mentee might even find themselves in reversed roles. Achieving this high level of mutual respect leads to close friendship, high levels of collegial support, and continuous shared learning experiences that improve effectiveness for both mentor and protégé.

Almost on My Own

Mentee Reflection: Jeromey

As I look back on everything that has happened since I began teaching, I am thankful and fortunate to be where I am. My love for children and the personal relationships I've established with students has made my experience memorable and fulfilling. Each day, I wake and commit to making a difference in the lives of my students. I am rewarded each day by the inspiration of their joyous conversations.

My mentor has been there when I needed him, guided me through many trials, and continues to help me establish goals. His example, knowledge, and shared experiences were a strong influence on my decision to become a principal. He's guided me through good times and bad and helped me achieve my goals.

Despite my experience, I still depend on my mentor for guidance and assurance when facing difficult decisions. I notice that lots of other effective principals also seek out their mentors when times are tough. But I'm feeling more independent, learning, acting more than reacting, and leading.

My mentor will always be an important part of my life. I will always look to him for guidance. I'm fortunate that early on he established clear guidelines for mentoring, set high expectations, willingly gave of his time, and wanted to learn as much as I did. Most importantly, Dustin, Paul, and I share a model of mentoring that is special, true to the theoretical models, and smoothly moving through the final phase leading toward self-sufficiency and productivity for each.

Mentee Reflection: Dustin

Jeromey and I share a love for children and education. I look forward to the exciting and new challenges each day provides, knowing I can affect a child, teacher, or parent in a positive way. Working to shape young minds and interacting daily with the children inspires me. Enabling *all* children to become successful is sometimes a long and challenging process, but the rewards are indescribable.

I have always been one who was extremely independent; however, as challenges presented themselves in my first principalship, I learned early on that I would have to budge and depend on someone for help. I realized the importance of a mentor. As much as I tried to be independent (maybe for fear that Paul would think I could not take the heat), I realized that to be successful as an administrator, I could not rely on my instincts and training alone. It took me a while before I began to call Paul and routinely communicate with him via phone calls, e-mails, and our weekly mentoring meetings.

The mentoring partnership that Paul, Jeromey, and I have established is priceless. Now, as colleagues, we work closely together and depend on each other for assistance almost daily. We are a team that has worked very hard on our "game plan," and it has paid off tremendously. Our relationship will continue long after Paul retires or we go our separate ways. We have established a friendly yet professional bond that fuels our desire to learn as principals and human beings, and the relationship will never end.

Success is not the key to happiness. Happiness is the key to success. If you love what you are doing, you will be successful.

—Albert Schweitzer

Changing habits is hard work. That's why making lasting change requires a strong commitment to a future vision of oneself—especially during stressful times or amid growing responsibilities.

—Daniel Goleman
from *Primal Leadership*

No one learns to make the right decisions without being free to make the wrong ones.

—Author Unknown

If my mind can conceive it, and my heart can believe it, then I can achieve it.

—Muhammed Ali

Part V

Mentoring Wisdom From Experts Around the Country

W hen I set out to serve as a mentor, I first relied upon my personal experiences and memories of how my own mentors had influenced me. Since then, I've continued to learn through reading extensively, writing, speaking, and trial and error. One of the most important learning paths of all for me has been conversation with respected colleagues. I've asked some of them here to share their own words of wisdom, tips, stories that still move them, and lessons learned. Some of these are consistent with what I've experienced, but all of them widen the lens on mentoring to include a wealth of experience from large and small districts across the country. Taken together and joined to our longer case study, they deeply enrich the startup knowledge of any new mentor. What follows is what has been generously shared by these mentoring colleagues.

ROSIE YOUNG, Principal, Watson Lane Elementary School, Louisville, KY

New principals must understand how to take the pulse of the instructional program in short amounts of time. Conducting classroom observations and following the established evaluation progress are important tasks and must be a priority among the myriad things a principal must do. Additionally, the new principal must understand the importance of the walk-through, having conversations with staff and students, and establishing a vision of high achievement for all students.

I think it is important for principals to look at all sides of an issue when making critical decisions. Understanding what the critical decisions are and what does not require a great deal of worry or concern is something every new principal must quickly learn. Mentors need to help, but not jump into a discussion too quickly with advice. Care must be taken to not always "tell" the new principal what to do but to guide him or her to examine options and select what is most beneficial.

The principalship is an isolated job, and the mentor's most important work is to make the protégé feel supported and competent. It is uplifting to assist colleagues and experience their gratitude. Mentors gain benefits from their protégés—enthusiasm, new perspectives, different life experiences and training, and a different set of priorities. These experiences can be very energizing!

Facing Poor Test Results in Kentucky

A new principal, faced with poor test scores, was planning to present data to the staff and develop a plan to raise scores. While talking with the new principal, we discussed the need to relate the information without placing blame on individual teachers or the students. With only a couple of months experience at the school, the new principal was just beginning to get a feel for the instructional program. We discussed the need to set the tone before the sharing of the data. Establishing trust among the staff was determined to be a critical part of the plan in setting the tone. The new principal truly wanted to assist with the academic growth of the school. She expressed a desire to become involved and play a key role in reshaping the instructional program. Therefore, on the day of the staff meeting, the new principal shared her vision along with the need for the school to become a learning community able to analyze data and move forward. While she continued to model her expectations for learning and growth, this meeting did a great deal to establish a strong partnership to increase the academic achievement of the students.

Tips for Mentors

Mentor principals can help protégés establish priorities, sort through the various demands, share shortcuts, work the system, and act as a sounding board. Additionally, mentors need to

- Establish trust and partnership,
- Share and discuss goals and needs of the mentoring relationship,
- Maintain confidentiality,
- Share mistakes you have made,
- Support decisions made by the new principal even if you would not have made that decision,
- Avoid criticizing the protégé to peers and colleagues,
- Share what you have learned from the protégé,
- Be accessible and establish procedures for making routine contact,
- Handle problem areas in a sensitive manner.

Mentoring principals needs to become an ongoing process with a prescribed plan. Mentors need to spend time with the protégé in her or his school to observe and provide feedback. Likewise, invite the protégé to observe you in a variety of situations and follow up with debriefing and reflection. There are a variety of inventories available that protégés may take to aid in their self-reflection. The mentor and protégé can use the results to determine priorities for growth and professional development. The mentoring relationship provides growth opportunities for both the mentor and protégé.

Mentors should also promote their protégé's active involvement in professional associations and activities. Attend professional meetings, workshops, and conferences together. Reflect afterwards. A strong mentoring relationship expands the collegial networks and mutual support systems for both the mentor and protégé. Establish a sense of openness and trust so that anything can be discussed and there are no silly questions. Share your personal successes and failures.

BONNIE LEW TRYON, Principal, Golding Elementary School, Cobleskill, NY

I believe the most effective mentoring strategy is to include the intern or new principal in as many actual day-to-day "real life" principal duties as possible. Observing rich conversations between practicing principals as they talk about their workday can provide great insights for a protégé. Listening and "soaking up" the content is a great learning experience.

Mentors need to help their protégés see the "big picture" on issues. Understanding how one decision affects another takes experience. Principals need experience, and at times intuition, to make those decisions work together.

Using Poetry to Enhance School Leadership

I like to use poetry and visuals to illustrate key points at faculty meetings. My mother was an English teacher and later a college professor, so I guess I learned my love of verse from her. I enjoy reading poetry aloud and I usually get good feedback when I do. Not so with everyone. My intern tried to imitate my use of poetry at a staff meeting and was not well received. He facilitated the staff meeting adequately, but learned he needed to be himself. Not everyone should read poetry!

We spent time reflecting about the faculty meeting. We agreed that it is not necessary, let alone desirable, for a new administrator to use leadership techniques and tools in the same way as the mentor. We each have our own style. Protégés need to adapt others' ideas and style and use what works for them in the most advantageous ways.

This point was best illustrated when the intern, during a later training class for teachers, used chart paper and markers in a very effective way—much more inventive than anything I could have thought to use. Mentoring is not about making a clone. Rather, it is about nurturing another to be comfortable and capable using his or her tools in an effective, unique manner.

Tips for Mentors

Mentors need to set aside a specific time on a regular basis to meet and share with their protégés. This allows the new principal to focus. He or she can count on a time to present issues and concerns. Setting aside a regular specific time also demonstrates that the new principal is valued and important. Time is precious. Giving quality time to a new colleague makes a strong statement about his or her contributions to the field. Establishing specific goals and priorities helps ensure success in the partnership.

Trust is important in any meaningful relationship, and it is a vital part in developing effective mentor/protégé partnerships. Participants must understand confidentiality and respect each other through their learning processes. Both must establish goals, identify boundaries, set clear expectations, and support each other through crises.

Young principals often enter the field believing they have "all the answers" and the courage to make changes in a school right away. My experience has been that unless the superintendent and the faculty are adamant that changes take place immediately, starting out a principalship by becoming a good listener and observer is usually the best recipe for success. Zealots don't often have longevity.

MARY KAY SOMMERS, Principal, Shepardson Elementary School, Fort Collins, CO

Principal mentors need to identify and prioritize what their protégés must learn and provide opportunities to remediate identified deficiencies. It helps to share experiences from areas of strength as well as weakness. Not only do protégés learn when mentors model their strengths, but other practicing principals will as well. Mentors need to be good listeners and encourage reflection. They can help their protégés by insightfully analyzing and explaining their thought processes when making a decision. Meeting regularly and discussing the decision-making process, reflecting, advising, and evaluating others' responses can be invaluable. Mentors can also aid with prioritizing the workload and dealing with difficult adult problems.

Implementing a Schoolwide Discipline Plan

As an administrative intern, my protégé accepted a project to implement a schoolwide discipline system. We were not experiencing excessive problems, but I had attended a workshop that intrigued me. I gained insights that had value for our common gathering areas as well as for individual teachers. She accepted the project with enthusiasm and started by attending a training session with a colleague. Afterwards, they created a team of teachers to consider this plan. Next, they visited schools that were using the program and compared notes. The committee, which the intern chaired, made a recommendation to the staff to implement this program. They designed the important parts of the plan to share with the staff and "sold" it. In the summer months that followed, the committee created the lessons for each area and placed them in a notebook. They prepared a "training" plan for the entire staff in August and taught them for a full day.

I asked her to reflect afterwards about what made it so successful. She described the high level of synergy as a new experience. The team was empowered to make the decisions and they generated incredible dialogue and remained focused. She also recognized the value of having diversity on the team, as the results incorporated the different strengths of each person. Everyone felt valued and enjoyed the process as well as the outcome.

This plan remains intact after three years with other team members now accepting the leadership role.

BOB KOENIGSKNECHT,
Retired Principal, Habel
Elementary School, Sterling Heights, MI

Mentoring is best accomplished by developing a caring, supportive, and trusting relationship with protégés. This means placing the emphasis on privacy and confidentiality. Both protégé and mentor understand that information they share remains with them. When that happens, a very open communication partnership develops and grows.

New principals grow and become the "instructional leader" when they utilize the strengths of their entire staff and empower them to help make positive changes in the school. Additionally, an effective instructional leader with a vision of an exemplary school knows to involve all members of the community. This includes all certified and noncertified personnel along with parents, students, and business and service groups in their community. To accomplish this awesome task, protégés are wise to join their professional associations and attend workshops and conferences. Learning from their mentors and others is ongoing. It is important to network with peers, read education journals and books, study best leadership practices, and take every opportunity to stay current on educational issues.

Mentors can have a big influence on the success of a new principal. The successful mentoring partnership is characterized by a positive and comfortable relationship involving trust, open communication, and respect for each other. Protégés know that their mentors are always available, person-to-person, by phone, or e-mail. Mentor and protégé meet in person and have an agenda when necessary. An agenda helps prioritize issues and concerns and keeps the meeting focused.

Mentors can coordinate meetings with different department personnel, other principals, and key leaders within a community. This is especially helpful in larger districts.

Mentors need to share ideas, suggestions, and experience. They need to patiently help protégés to reflect on their own leadership skills. They need to emphasize that leading people is all about influence and that the development of positive people skills is critical to their success as a leader. Mentors also enable their protégés to become effective leaders when they help them become effective listeners, communicators, and accessible and visible to the entire community. Mentors discuss the importance of planning, creating a happy school environment, maintaining a love for children, and keeping a sense of humor.

Eliminating Morning Recess

One of my protégés informed me that my suggestion to be an effective observer and avoid making too many changes her first year as principal proved to be good advice. This protégé considered eliminating morning recess in the middle of the year in order to increase instructional time for students. She had a great idea. Her idea to improve student achievement by increasing instructional time was very admirable. However, while listening to her, I felt she did not have enough support to make the change. I advised her to wait until the beginning of the next school year while using the remainder of the school term to solicit support and involve all staff in the development and implementation of the plan. She generously used the suggestion and everything worked very well. Timing and getting support for sensitive issues are critical for building trust and ownership by staff.

Learning to "Pick Your Battles"

It was the second day of school. A parent had called and insisted on talking with the principal at 10:00 a.m. I was also scheduled to meet with her at that time and had arrived a few minutes early. I was unaware that the parents of a student had insisted on meeting with my protégé. When I entered the school office, my protégé looked at me and said, "I'm so glad to see you." She told me of the concern the parents had regarding their child. They wanted their child removed from a particular classroom because they did not approve of the teacher. My protégé indicated to me that she had already spoken with the parents on two occasions and given them a good rationale for not changing classrooms. I suggested that this might be a case where she needed to "pick her battles." I indicated that after two conferences, if the parents were still persistent about the change, it might be time to consider the request.

The parents soon arrived. I visited other people in the building until the conference ended. My protégé and I met and debriefed after the parents left the building. She said the parents were upset and came with a threatening letter addressed to the superintendent. When my protégé indicated she had decided to honor the parents' request for the change, the tone of the conference improved. My protégé asked for the parents' future support, and the conference ended on a positive note.

Every situation is different. Effective leaders need to know when to be flexible and when to hold their ground. Good leaders learn how to pick their battles.

LYNN BABCOCK, Retired
Principal/Past President of NAESP,
Grant Elementary School, Livonia, MI

Effective principals who make the best mentors are available, supportive and encouraging. They nurture teacher leaders to consider the principalship. They see the potential and best qualities in others. They become supportive, good listeners, and stand ready to give advice if needed or when asked.

Mentors often continue to reap the benefits of the partnerships years after they first began. Not only do protégés become colleagues and close working associates, but the friendships that develop during the mentoring partnership last for years, even lifetimes.

SUSAN VAN ZANT, Retired
Middle School Principal,
Meadowbrook Middle School, Poway, CA

The staff at one elementary school was among the most senior in the district. Under the direction of a supportive principal, Mary, they were well organized and professional in their approach to learning. They were highly involved in school decisions and encouraged to reach beyond the walls of the school to share their expertise with others. The reading specialist had published a book, and two teachers were working on another soon-to-be-published reading strategy book. One teacher served on a national social studies committee. Eight other teachers frequently made presentations about their effective classroom practices. The staff was proud of student achievement and the school had received state and national recognition for its efforts. The PTA also had a fine record of achievement and was recognized as one of the top ten in the state of California. Mary was subsequently transferred to a middle school.

The district replaced her with Jane, a principal from a school with a highly mobile student and staff population. Most of the teachers at Jane's previous school were new to teaching. She was used to making decisions without staff involvement and did not appreciate being questioned. Soon after the announcement of her new assignment, one of Jane's first actions was to change some classroom and grade level assignments. As the year progressed, the staff perceived that she played "favorites" with the new teachers and she did not follow through on commitments. In the course of two years, things went from bad to worse. Some of the most respected teachers decided to transfer to other schools. The remaining teachers were unhappy and the PTA disliked the fact that she did not appear to support their programs. The third year was no better. After the local television news showed parents picketing in front of the school, and teachers spoke out against the principal at a school board meeting, the district transferred her to the district office.

Given a one-day notice, another principal, David, was assigned to this school. He walked in the door, looked at the blank faces of the staff, went to his office and called me. He was unhappy being at this school where everyone had a negative attitude. We discussed the history of the school. Based upon the fact that the teachers and PTA were once considered to be exemplary and highly supportive, I suggested that he grab his pencil and a pad of paper and visit every classroom for a brief period of time. When he left the room he would leave a positive note on the desk of each teacher. The next day he would hold a staff meeting where he would ask the staff to set goals for the school year and he would listen without judgment to anything they had to say. During the next few months, David and I talked frequently about ways to involve teachers in decision making and how he could support PTA efforts. Six months later the school was renewed. David was happy he had been reassigned.

Tips for Principals

- To gain a perspective about the school, principals new to the site should make every effort to contact the previous principal. Often successful procedures are in place.
- In the first year, it is wise for a principal to go slowly. Making unneeded drastic changes can lead to poor staff morale.
- Principals should never play favorites. All staff members should be treated with fairness, dignity, and respect.
- It is important to support the parent-teacher organization. Parents, in turn, will support school programs.
- It is important to support all teachers. Teachers, like everyone else, respond to positive reinforcement.

When You Don't Understand, Call Your Mentor

Soon after Ed was assigned to his first principalship, he was given a budget printout. He had previous experience with budgets and he believed he understood the various funds and categories.

Subsequently he was invited to attend a meeting at the district presented by the head accountant. When he returned, he immediately called me and asked if I could come to his office. It seems that the accountant "talked only in numbers." "You cannot move the 4310s from the general fund to the categorical programs such as 377-068 without prior approval, but you can move the 5712s to the 377-780." He returned with pages of notes. When I walked in the door he handed me the notes and stated, "I don't know what to do." After looking at the notes, I realized that the accountant had presented a generic presentation. Much of what he said had to do with different departments such as transportation, publications, and food services.

Ed and I sat down and carefully went over his budget and he made notes on the procedure and forms he needed to complete. We reviewed the difference between transferring funds and charges among and between the various programs. The next month when his budget printout arrived we again analyzed his budget. He now understands the various categories, programs, and funds and is well able to manage his budget.

Tips for Principals

- Every district seems to have unique budget forms and procedures. Principals new to a district should interact with a seasoned principal in order to learn how to effectively navigate through the paperwork.
- Principals new to a site should seek a mentor. The assistance of a seasoned principal can be invaluable.

KATIE MATHEWS, Principal, Park Elementary School, Kearney, NE

As I have mentored other principals I have been able to share ideas that work for other people and myself for expanding leadership capacity in a school that focuses on learning. One idea that I "stole" from my mentors was the development of leadership teams (rather than committees) for school improvement. Those leadership teams are given the important roles of examining student learning data, selecting school improvement goals, researching possible strategies, and developing a plan. Each leadership team has a staff member who serves as the chair. All staff members are encouraged to participate in teams.

I've shared with each principal I mentored a process used to involve the staff in leadership at our school. Each was encouraged to make it fit his or her personal style and the culture of his or her school. The key points of the process are as follows:

- Set up a time to sit down with each certified and classified staff member to get to know him or her, ask questions, identify school strengths and weaknesses, and determine what needs to be developed
- Find out what kind of personal and professional support people need from the principal
- Find time at the beginning of the year for a staff retreat. Set the tone from the beginning that learning is the most important issue
- Set forth your expectations and vision for the school
- Throughout the year, spend time at staff meetings focusing on items that relate to the vision of the school
- Place the mission and vision statement on each agenda and staff and parent communication

It is important when mentoring principals to stay focused on learning rather than management issues. I encourage each mentee to read Rick DuFour's *The Principal as Staff Developer.* A gift I like to give to a new principal that covers everything is *The Elementary Principal's Complete Handbook* by Fred and Carol Chernow. My mentor gave it to me with an inspiring note in front.

Our calling to lead learning organizations is very challenging and can be defeating. Mentoring is going to be critical not only for new principals but seasoned principals as well, as the job changes daily and annually. When one mentors, the mentor is likely to learn more from the relationship than the mentee. What a tremendous privilege it is to lift up our profession and grow professionally at the same time!

MARK WHITE, Principal, Hintgen Elementary School, La Crosse, WI

In both cases, my protégés were members of my staff. After working with me as teachers and being mentored by me through their administration classes, they both obtained positions as elementary school principals in the state.

We often discussed the trivial managerial duties we need to get past in order to get on to the central issues of importance. We tried to find ways to shorten discussion of those issues and concentrate on student learning. Both benefited from participating in our school-based decision-making team and used that model when they moved to their new positions.

My protégés' biggest challenge, causing them the most concern, was the development of relationships with their new staff. Both were young principals working with very experienced staffs. They needed to demonstrate their knowledge, insights, and determination right away. We spent time talking about the related challenges. I tried to be a ready ear and source of information to help them get off to the best start possible. Communication and a trusting relationship were key to our successful mentoring partnership.

It is not easy to let someone else deal with your personal issues or walk in your shoes—either from the perspective of the mentor or mentee. Teachers may think they want to become administrators, but until they experience the realities, they won't know. We demand that teachers have a mentor as they begin working with children—it is only natural that we would expect the same for principals.

JANE ELLEN BOULTINGHOUSE,
Principal, Parkview Elementary
School, Columbus, IN

Looking back, I would help the protégé learn to put students first. The principal's paperwork is important, but not more important than the daily student and teacher contact. Set professional as well as personal goals for you and your school to achieve for the year. Always make time for your family. School can take a lot of your time, but remember, you have a life after work. You have to find a balance so everyone will feel they are a part of your life. It is also the "little things" that people remember. Take care of both families—the one at home and the one at school. Principals must realize that they are not only the leader of a building, but also a counselor, mechanic, crowd control specialist, and solver of all problems.

A Mentoring Moment That Made a Difference

I had a teacher completing an internship with me. She was amazed at the number of decisions a principal makes within a ten-minute period. But I hadn't thought much about that, since making rapid decisions becomes a routine part of being a leader. Now the intern is starting her fifth year as a principal. I called her on her opening day of school and reminded her of her observation many years back. I wished her a good school year and told her to keep making those decisions. She fought back tears and said I had made her day and couldn't believe I could remember that moment we shared. I think mentoring is a lifelong experience, not just done in one year or two.

Tips for Mentors

Admit your mistakes. There are no wrong answers, only challenges and concerns. Take time for yourself, and be "green"—always willing to learn. The motto should be "as good as I am, how can I get better?"

MARY GRANT, Principal, Takoma Elementary School, Washington, DC

I have had the task of planning and providing training for new principals. I can't believe it. In addition to running my own school, I've enjoyed the challenges of being a principal mentor—experiences that have occurred beyond my school.

My first step was to make the new principals feel comfortable and to let them know that we are in this together and that DCAESP will continue to be there for them. I provided a PowerPoint presentation and samples of forms and letters that I use with my staff. I also walked them through what the year may look like. While this is also the task of the assistant superintendent, I felt that our organization could make a major contribution in assisting new principals. The new principals feel that by providing them with useful materials we really help them to stay afloat. Being available when they need to ask questions has also been a plus for them.

Tips for New Principals

A few key points given to new principals on arriving at their new school:

- If possible, meet with the outgoing principal to make the transition a smooth one for the new administrator and the entire school community.

- Meet with the head custodian and tour the facility to determine needs.

- Meet with office staff to discuss their job descriptions and roles.

- Have an audit conducted of school financial records immediately.

- Change locks on the office door and any other important areas.

- Meet with key leaders and stakeholders of the school community.

- Meet with community members and business partners renewing their partnerships, and acquaint them with the new administration.

It is very important that the mentor demonstrate an ability to support the new principal. An assigned mentor who does not have the ability to help a new principal is a disaster waiting to happen. Providing assistance and allowing the new principal to call when in need of help provides a comfort level between the mentor and protégé. It is important to return calls to the protégé in a timely manner. It is also important for protégés to see their mentor in action. This experience provides them with tools that can help them be more at ease with their task.

Every principal must know the *Union Contract and Board Rules.* New principals are the new kids on the block and will be tested by students, teachers, and parents. Once they have some crises under their belt and experience following the policies, a major part of the battle is over. The research supports that bargaining organizations can be a thorn in the side of administrators if contractual rules are not adhered to properly. The new principal needs to totally understand the process for a grievance or filing a complaint.

Once the protégé has gained confidence under the mentor's guidance, professional respect is imminent. The protégé will likely develop higher levels of trust with his or her mentor than anyone else. Mentors have to teach new administrators how to pick and choose their battles. Help them learn which ones are not worth their time. You want to encourage protégés to participate in professional organizations that stimulate and encourage their professional and personal growth. A key piece of advice is for the mentor to refrain from telling the protégé how to run his or her school, but instead to guide him or her towards effective leadership practices. A good mentor recommends when asked and has a large listening ear.

The Mentor's Response to Emergency Situations

On the first day of school, I received a frantic phone call from a principal who sounded very upset. Of course, I immediately stopped to answer the call. She stated that she had an irate adult running through her building and she could not get her out. I stated that first she must be calm, demonstrating good control tactics to all those in the building. I told her to calmly make an announcement to all staff members requesting that they step to their doors and watch for an unauthorized person who is in the building. The announcement should request that the staff please contact the office if they locate this person. In the meantime, I suggested she call the police and request that security personnel thoroughly patrol the building. Later that day, the principal called to thank me for assisting her with the matter and report that the police removed the person from the building.

Reflections on Mentoring

Mentoring has been exciting, productive, and very much worth the time invested. As a mentor, I not only provide assistance to new and future administrators, I enhance my own personal and professional growth. The mentoring experience is a two-way learning experience. I help and I learn. Mentoring has afforded me the opportunity to reach many administrators from many sections of the city and provide them with guidance, resources, and most of all a little bit of faith that they can do well. After all, the point of mentoring is to decrease the attrition of administrators in education, and increase the number that enjoy their work and will add to the district's productivity.

MICHELLE PECINA, Principal, James Monroe Elementary School, Madera, CA

During the past two years, I have been involved with the California Network of School Leadership Coaches. I was trained by Gary Bloom and Associates from The New Teacher Center at the California State University in Santa Cruz. These sessions were expertly done, with many opportunities to view principals being coached on video as well as opportunities to practice. The balanced approach was emphasized. They taught us to balance being facilitative and instructional, depending on the situation.

My mentoring perspective has been evolving over the past two years as I have coached two new principals in my school district of Madera Unified. I volunteered to do so and believe, overall, the experience to be a successful one. The principals both see my role as a validator and an encourager.

The main priority I have is to ease the stress of being a new principal. The listening and problem-solving opportunities through regularly scheduled meetings have given the new principal an avenue to discuss real needs.

One of the principals wanted to approach the second year with a plan to ease tensions regarding an impending school remodeling project. We had previously discussed the importance of positive school climate, and the principal knew that something special had to happen to ease tensions. She had each staff member make a "crazy hat" at their first meeting. They all agreed to put on their hats on a day when the remodeling blues hit, so they could signal each other that it was a frustrating day for them and take it with a little humor. This idea worked very well, and they all got through the remodeling in good spirits.

One lesson learned is that all school systems are not ready to embrace coaching for their principals because of the newness of the efforts. I would hope that the successes of teacher mentoring will spill over into the school administration ranks, but that has yet to be researched.

Tips for Mentors

Set up a regular schedule to meet and document the times. Use a simple form to record the meeting (e.g., good things happening, problems to be addressed, resources, next steps). Both mentor and mentee should keep copies. Encourage and validate.

Part VI

Reflections on the Most Important Aspects of Mentoring

In this section, the authors reflect from their separate mentor and mentee perspectives on the value of mentoring, the primary benefits, and keys and paths to professional growth in the principalship.

Since becoming a principal, what are the most significant things you've learned that have surprised you about the job?

DUSTIN: The most surprising aspect of this job is the number of demands placed upon you. You really can't fathom the amount of work that goes into this job until you are in the position. The first week of my first job I couldn't believe how many questions the teachers had for me. That was the most difficult thing to get used to.

JEROMEY: The most significant thing that I have learned this first year is how important it is to manage time and plan ahead. Principals are pulled in many directions and have so much on their plate. I've had to learn how to balance my time and give the most attention to things that make the most impact on the students and our school. Central office obligations and deadlines also are a priority and need to take precedence over many things at the building level. Many days there are things that happen that I never expect, and when this happens, I've learned to prioritize and quickly find solutions so that I can finish important tasks.

PAUL: Despite all the literature about the important role a principal plays in instructional leadership, he or she still must always focus on management responsibilities. Even after 17 years, much of my routine day continues to be consumed by management tasks. The job is almost impossible for one person to adequately perform. If the buses don't run, schedules need adjusting, food isn't good, or student discipline gets out of hand, the problems eventually surface in my office for me to deal with. There are days when I can never find time away from the phone, talking with parents, attending meetings, or performing district-related assignments, to spend quality time with teachers and students in classrooms. Paperwork continues to pile on my desk and require attention, despite my experienced ability to handle things only once. I recognize the importance of my role as an instructional leader, but like most principals without any assistance, the battle to find time continues to be a major challenge.

I've also learned that nothing effective can happen in an elementary or middle level school without the endorsement and support of the principal. Given my support and involvement, any staff member's initiative can get off the ground and flourish. Without it, the project is doomed. The responsibility for effective programs requires great time commitment and knowledge from the principal. Juggling all the responsibilities becomes overwhelming for many principals, especially beginners. Regardless, effective, comprehensive schools have numerous support services and special programs—all endorsed and supported by the principal. I've never been content with status quo, and if there is a good program that will benefit the children in my school, I want it implemented!

Another significant observation is the amount of conflict that can be generated with collective bargaining groups when trying to implement change. This block requires principals, as middle managers, to tread lightly and continuously find ways to move around union mediocrity. Although they are most accountable for their school's results, principals are the least protected. In those cases where the community insists that an ineffective teacher be dismissed, after lengthy evaluations and collection of evidence, the process often focuses on the principal's evaluation and due process technicalities. Too often, conflict becomes so great that the principal becomes expendable. This scenario frightens most principals, and as a result, few choose to act on challenges of which they are well aware, for their own protection and job security.

My experience shows that more than being managers and instructional leaders, principals must also be *leaders*. The No Child Left Behind Act and other state and federal mandates require increased levels of accountability from principals. Timelines to produce results and adequate yearly progress now require principals to immediately raise serious, sensitive questions about curriculum and instruction, as well as teacher performance, that before could be addressed over several years. Attitudes and deep-seated beliefs about student learning must be challenged. Learning how to lead change, above and beyond managing and instructional leadership, is the next critical hurdle for school leaders.

What is the most difficult aspect of the job? The most rewarding?

DUSTIN: The most difficult part of being a principal is not having enough time. There are so many things for a principal to do and not enough time to do them. If you are a perfectionist (or try to be) like me, this can drive you crazy! I want to get everything done each day, but it is impossible. To be an effective principal, you must manage your time wisely and learn to prioritize your tasks. My favorite thing is to greet the children and visit them throughout the day. This is top on my list, although it takes about an hour or two away from important paperwork. The paperwork waits! I have learned that to manage my way, I have to be on top of things in advance. This is the only way for me to be successful.

The most rewarding part of my job is being with the children and parents. I love a nice challenge from a parent. When I am able to be a problem solver and make others happy, it really makes me feel good about what I do. To help others gives me a natural high that fuels my intentions. In a way, I feel like a father—someone for the children to look up to, and sometimes also for the teachers as well.

JEROMEY: The most difficult part of my job has been the trial and error process. I have learned so much this year but done some pretty rookie things along the way. I've had to stop and assess my position, call others and even apologize due to my "I think I'm right and you're wrong" approaches.

The most rewarding part of the year has come from the programs and successful changes that I've experienced in the school. It's a great feeling when you implement something and see that a positive impact has been made. To see students and staff grow, as well as experiencing personal growth, is what education is all about. When you see these things happening, you know you accomplished your purpose—to teach.

PAUL: People development is an ongoing issue for principals as they work to create change in order to continuously improve their staffs. The essential knowledge and theory offered in college and university preparatory programs is no longer enough to prepare entry-level teachers for the real world of the classroom. The media does not portray education in a favorable light, and the best and the brightest high school graduates too frequently choose other career options. Shortages further complicate the supply and demand as principals scramble to hire the best people.

Principals must be master motivators, model adult learning, and influence others to change behaviors and reach increasingly higher levels of effectiveness. Staff development must be ongoing and supported over time. High stakes testing and limited budgets are negatively impacting principals' abilities to provide effective inservice and staff development opportunities. Finding time and money for adult learning is extremely difficult, but necessary.

It is most rewarding to see the "lights in the eyes" of students as they learn from inspirational teachers. Principals pursue their jobs because they have a passion for helping others learn, grow, and improve the quality of their lives—both students and adults.

After six long years leading a school to transform its poor self-esteem and low performance, like music to my ears, I can hear the cheers of my staff as I announced on the last day of school that they had achieved the highest district reading scores in 1st, 4th, and 6th grades. It may never be repeated, but that achievement was among the most rewarding and memorable of my career.

Since becoming a principal, what are the most significant things you've learned by participating as a mentee?

DUSTIN: Through the mentoring opportunities with Paul, I've learned a lot of important lessons. I've learned that it is definitely lonely at the top, and you must have a network of principals and administrators to contact for advice, help, and friendships. As I look back on my first two years as a principal, I can't begin to imagine how much tougher it would have been without a veteran principal helping and guiding me through difficult situations. I've learned that no matter how well you think you are doing, you always need to discuss ideas and issues with other professionals. Networking is crucial to being a quality administrator.

Networking is crucial to being a quality administrator.

—Dustin D. Knight

Another thing I've learned from Paul is that although Jeromey, he, and I don't always agree on everything, we still have a professional and personal relationship that helps each other grow. Accepting advice and ideas from others is the most important thing a new administrator can do. Don't be too proud to ask for help. I tried at first, but it only made things more stressful. Find a good mentor and establish a strong working relationship that will foster and support your administrative goals.

JEROMEY: There are many things that I've learned as a protégé. Sharing a mentor with others has given me the opportunity to know that I have a network of new principals that I can talk with. I've learned how important it is to think ahead and meet deadlines. Another important thing that I have learned is that it is vital to make sure things are clearly explained to staff, parents, and students. Communication is one of the most important skills a principal should have.

How have you learned these things and how have you benefited from the mentor-mentee relationship?

DUSTIN: As mentioned previously, I have learned a great deal from Paul and Jeromey during our mentoring breakfasts. This has been the best opportunity for us to get together, meet, and talk about our busy weeks. I honestly don't think I would be the principal that I am today without Paul Young's help. He has been a true mentor, providing rigorous yet superior guidance. I've learned that to be successful in this profession, you must have someone to show you the ropes correctly.

JEROMEY: I'm able to talk with someone about what I'm experiencing and ask for suggestions on how I can or could have approached important decisions. Without a mentor for support, guidance, and ideas, I'm not sure how I could have made it through this first year. Communicating ideas, sharing suggestions, and being a critical friend is what this relationship is all about.

PAUL: Knowing that I have eyes watching everything I do, listening when I speak, and second-guessing all my actions, I am working harder than ever to be the very best model I can be. I have raised my self-expectations and reflected on the "art" of being a principal more than I ever had before. I enjoy learning again. Being a mentor allows me to focus on teaching and learning.

As much as I focus on nurturing my protégés, I am excited by what I learn by observing them. When they succeed, I can see the positive results of my influence and instruction, and it is a source of great pride. When they fail, I suffer privately with them. I reflect and evaluate how I could have prepared them better. But as much as I give, I receive just as much in return. They've taught me things I never knew, particularly about technology. When we talk about personnel issues, I learn by observing them interacting and taking different approaches with people, contrary to what I might have selected. Sharing has enabled the development of a strong partnership. I enjoy having a willing ear when I need to vent. I appreciate having confidants and colleagues I can completely trust. Mentoring has renewed my passion for the principalship, enhanced my leadership potential, and become a source of pride.

What would you do differently if you were to begin your principalship again? How would you design your mentor-mentee relationship differently? What would you want the mentor to do differently? What would you do differently?

DUSTIN: If I were to begin my principalship again, I would probably increase communications with my mentor and other colleagues. When I first started as a principal, I thought I could run the school and learn from my mistakes without talking a lot about them. I was wrong. I remember becoming very stressed out during the first three months of my first job. The stress was eating me up inside, and I didn't do what I should have done—call my mentor more frequently. I think maybe I was afraid that I would disappoint him by asking him too much. I've always been a very independent person. It was hard to break away from this "independent" way of thinking.

The relationship that I now have with Paul and Jeromey is very good. We are like three close friends and colleagues who can share and discuss our professional and personal challenges. I wouldn't change a thing, except I would like to have Paul pay for every breakfast since he makes more money than the two of us!

If the mentor (Paul) would change anything, I think I would like him to not push us so hard. Yet, the more I think of this, the more I am glad he does. Jeromey and I are the principals we are because of Paul pushing us and helping us reach our fullest potential.

JEROMEY: If I had to do this year all over again, I would have made sure that I took time to meet with teachers and would have done a better job of being a listener. I would also have spent more time on details and doing a better job of communicating ideas and school goals.

I would probably have been more honest about how I felt throughout the year. There were many times when, if I had opened up a little, I might have been able to get a better answer for a situation.

I think it would have helped if my mentor knew that we have totally different leadership styles and could have looked at things through my eyes. Things that work with him will not work for me. I now need suggestions for how I can approach things rather than directions for how it should be done.

PAUL: If I were to begin the principalship again, I would read and learn more about the mentoring process. I could have benefited from knowing the expectations of a protégé. I thought only of myself, never giving consideration to the needs of my mentor. I experienced support from a good mentor, but our relationship developed naturally as friends. There is more to effective mentoring than we instinctively experienced with each other in 1986.

In fact, many mentors have influenced my professional career—but I never thought of the important people in my life as mentors when we were together. There have always been mentors, but it seems only in recent years that mentoring has received proper attention and value as a support system—but mostly for beginning teachers. Principal mentoring needs continued research, standards, formalization, widespread support, dedicated time, financial resources, and implementation in school districts across the nation.

To do it again, my mentoring relationship would be more structured, involve regular times to meet and reflect, and be evaluated by pre-established objectives. I know now that I would have benefited from established time to reflect and question my mentor. Mentoring within close proximity is beneficial. Trust is an important part of the partnership. I developed a trusting relationship, but if I could relive history, I would become a more active participant in developing trust with my mentor more rapidly than was experienced.

What kind of support is most important and valuable to you?

DUSTIN: I really like having support on tough issues. I don't need someone to tell me I'm doing a great job all of the time. Instead, I would like to know what I need to do to continue to improve. I will always have room to improve whether in my second year or thirtieth year as a principal. When I have an irate parent, or a difficult student problem, or even a teacher's union issue, I like knowing that I can call Paul and he will talk me through it because he's been there before. Paul isn't afraid to tell you what he would do or suggest what needs to be done in a specific situation. Support is crucial to your success as a principal.

JEROMEY: The best support that I had was the knowledge that I could pick up the phone and ask questions. Answers to important questions have been a big help this year. Mentoring breakfasts have also helped to reflect on the week and to prepare for the next. Learning how to access and use resources within the district and knowing where to go outside for answers has made a difference and saved time.

PAUL: I grow most from my collection of close critical friends who will "tell me like it is" when I need it most. Those critical friends include my family and a widespread network of professional colleagues. For one to become my critical friend, I must regard them with the utmost respect. I have a series of informal tests by which I assess our developing relationship, and those who prove most reliable become my closest confidants and friends. I would do anything for these individuals.

I need regular contact with positive, ambitious, competitive people. I gain nothing and become very frustrated with those with whom I must work hard to support any relationship. My circle of friends must invigorate, encourage, and motivate me. I enjoy people with a sense of humor who can take it but also give it back.

Describe your mistakes, how you handled them, and what you've learned.

DUSTIN: I am usually pretty focused and over-prepared; however, when I slack off, it catches up to me very fast. This happens rarely, but when it does, I pay dearly. Usually when I make a mistake, I try to correct it as quickly as it happens. I tend to look at my mistakes as learning experiences. If everything was perfect all of the time, I wouldn't be able to grow professionally and personally. I've learned that you must be on top of your game at all times. The staff looks to you for answers, guidance, and leadership, and if you don't perform, they will notice. Making mistakes isn't always bad; however, you must learn from them and not repeat them.

JEROMEY: I have made so many mistakes this year, but learned something from each one.

- I've learned to think through things when possible, and if there is not enough time, find it. Time is precious. In many situations you need to be creative when it comes to buying time. This may be as simple as shutting the door to think or picking up the telephone for ideas.
- I've learned that each person on your staff has different needs, and if you change something for one, you might upset a lot more. There are many personalities on my staff. Each person has certain needs and visions of what they would like to have happen in the school. At first I tried to meet each person's needs, until I realized that I wasn't leading. The needs of the school must be consistently what is best for the students and the district, not individuals.
- I've learned that sometimes you need to be patient and other times being patient may make things worse. Sometimes it is important to take your time and listen to teachers. You need to be understanding, yet at other times you need to be tough. When you are only

a problem solver and listener, people can take advantage. Things can stall. It's important to be a leader and communicate your expectations to people.

- I've learned who I can trust with anything and who I don't trust with important information. Be careful what you say and more careful whom you say it to. Find someone you know will keep a secret; then you can be truly open with that person.
- I've learned that sharing too much information sometimes can be dangerous.
- I've also learned that not sharing information can be dangerous. Sharing information is a very important part of being a leader. It's deciding what information and with whom you share that can be tricky. Only share what you think others can be trusted to know. Make sure the information is clear enough that it can't be taken out of context if shared with others.
- I've learned that staying calm under fire is usually best, but at times can appear weak. Pick your battles and act accordingly. I've learned that I am the leader in the school and all eyes are on me. My reactions to situations are what separates me from others. Whatever I say or do will almost always be discussed, whether I know it or not.
- I've learned that to have a successful team you need to be a successful leader. The most important part of a team is the coach and then its players.
- I've learned to delegate authority and keep the monkeys off my back. Whenever possible, find someone to help and empower them to lead.

PAUL: As a mentor, I've often been too forceful and direct. I am too quick to criticize. I lack patience. I get very frustrated when my protégés don't perform to meet my expectations, and I become angry and overly self-critical when I realize that my inadequate teaching led to their misunderstanding my expectations.

My leadership style is that of a driver. I am very organized and task-oriented. My expectations are extremely high, especially for those closest to me whom I realize have the greatest potential. I have a high energy level and manage several projects simultaneously. I become frustrated when my protégés choose alternate leadership styles that I think will be ineffective. I have to hold my tongue to avoid the "I told you so" putdown. I am not always as professional as I attempt to teach them to be.

I am learning patience and working to choose the appropriate time to be critical. I've learned to allow my protégés to experience failure and learn lessons the hard way. I cannot protect them from everything.

Describe your successes, how you handled them, and what you've learned.

DUSTIN: Like Jeromey, I am the first person in my family to earn my bachelor's and master's degrees. I've never been one to toot my own horn. I am humble, but proud of my accomplishments. I'm proud to have become an elementary school principal at the age of 27. These are huge successes to me. I perceive myself as a "self-made man." I began working at the age of 14 and haven't stopped since. Working my way through high school and college, growing up in a broken home, and meeting challenges head on, has made me a strong, goal-oriented person. I know what it's like to be poor. I know what it's like not to have food or clothes in your house. I know what it's like to live with a single parent. I know what it's like to grow up not knowing how bad you had it until you became an adult. I know what it's like to have to work for everything I own. However frustrating it has been for me to see others have things handed to them, it only makes me appreciate everything I have that much more. I've earned everything I own—not because my parents didn't help me, but because they couldn't.

The other success that I enjoy is my family. I am probably prouder of my beautiful wife, Gina, and our two children, Chloe and Spencer, than anything else in my life. My career is wonderful, but my family comes second to none. My family is what keeps me going. I strive to provide them with the things I didn't have growing up. That doesn't mean I will spoil my children, but I want them to be well cared for. My children will still learn to appreciate everything they have—even if they have to start working at 14!

JEROMEY: Every day I find successes in what I do. Each day I try something new or make one more connection with a student. Every day I try to learn something that will help me professionally and make me a better principal. I try not to make a big deal out of my successes, but on the other hand, if I catch someone doing something good I make a big deal out of that.

PAUL: My successes have been realized from teaching, influencing, and observing these two protégés learn and lead the schools in a capable manner.

What have you identified from the mentor-mentee relationship that you have turned into a personal or professional goal, and why?

DUSTIN: I have identified the importance of continuing to grow professionally in my career no matter how long I have been at it. I see and work with Paul Young often. He has been a great mentor to me. He helps Jeromey and me when we need it. He offers support or chastises us when necessary. But one thing I've noticed about him that I like is that he listens and accepts ideas from us. He isn't too "old" to fear trying new things. Even though we are his mentees and lack his experience, he asks us for our opinions, and we teach him new things often.

Paul is very good at implementing change. In my short career, I've noticed that many people do not like change. Thinking of change reminds me of the book *Who Moved My Cheese?*, that Paul asked us to read. Although Paul is as old as my father, he is willing to change and roll with the punches. I've identified with this, and I think that is what has helped Paul be so successful in his career. My grandfather always told me, "The only thing permanent is change." This is so true, and it didn't really make much sense to me until I became a principal and observed an older gentleman (Paul) able to change and adapt to new ideas and situations.

JEROMEY: Anything that I learn from the mentor-mentee relationship that can make me a better principal becomes a professional goal. My mentor has introduced me to many people, and I try to learn as much as I can from others.

PAUL: Every practicing principal is encouraged to identify five aspiring principals, nurture them, and guide and support them through their administrative training courses and internship. But then they must become trusting mentors, help them acquire a good job, and ensure that their protégés become confidently established as effective principals in their own right. Once practicing principals have "their five" securely established in the profession, they have my permission to retire.

What advice do you have for others?

DUSTIN: Find a great mentor or a group of mentors that can help you through any tough times. Everyone will experience some difficult situations, and you must have someone to call for advice or just to vent. Be careful who you trust, but always remember the Education 101 rule, "Everything you do you should do for the children."

JEROMEY: I would encourage others to find people that help them grow professionally. After you find that person, try to learn as much as you can from him or her and take advantage of what he or she can offer you professionally. As long as he or she pushes you to do your best, chances are that you'll be headed in the right direction.

PAUL: All participants benefit from an effective, trusting mentor-mentee relationship. Both the mentor and the mentee have responsibilities to maintain in a partnership. These can be taught and learned. Learn from others' experiences. Talk via the phone, meet face-to-face, and reflect with your mentee regularly. Don't let disagreements fester too long. If both participants can't accept criticism and make a long-term commitment to learning, the relationship must change. Effective mentoring is a multi-year partnership, and the best continue for life.

SUMMARY AND CONCLUSIONS

As an undergraduate student preparing to be a teacher, I also aspired to be an elementary principal. I set this goal and achieved it at a young age. Little did I know how I would be supported in my new role through a positive and meaningful mentoring relationship. Through all of the ups and downs of my work, I have learned something daily. Some experiences, as I've shared, have been positive, others negative, scary, and very stressful, but through my mentoring with Paul Young and friendship with Jeromey Sheets, it has been much easier to cope, grow, and move forward as an administrator.

Whether it was the time spent at mentoring breakfasts or our phone calls to each other, the support from mentoring and networking has been a genuine success. It is crucial for the success of beginning administrators to identify a good mentor who will guide and help them through their first or even the tenth year of the principalship.

I like to use the analogy of a team. As an athlete, it has always been easy for me to understand that to accomplish more, team members must work together. The common saying goes, "There is no 'I' in TEAM." This is very true. You can't score a touchdown with one teammate. You can't accomplish as much by yourself as you can with a team. Jeromey, Paul, and I (as well as many other colleagues) are a team that works together toward one basic goal—improving student achievement.

Being a principal is not an easy job. It probably never has been and never will be. I listen to many principals who plan to retire or leave their jobs because of the continuing new challenges that face them. A principal must be a father or mother, counselor, leader, teacher, manager, doctor, friend, and so on. The list goes on and on, and the demands continue to build. New standardized testing mandates, an increasing number of single parent families, and the multitude of issues that principals must handle every day make the principalship an undesirable position for many. I clearly understand the demands placed upon me. I have the support of a great mentor who has prepared me for what I have met, stood beside me when needed, and doesn't plan to abandon me now.

Although being a principal is challenging, it is one of the most rewarding jobs available (next to teaching). Never underestimate the importance of establishing a strong meaningful relationship with a mentor who will go above and beyond to help. I thank Dr. Paul Young for his dedication and eagerness to help Jeromey and me learn and grow to become successful elementary principals. It takes a good friend, coach, teacher, and mentor to become successful. These words describe what Paul has been in my life.

Dustin D. Knight
Lancaster, Ohio

As I complete my first year as an elementary principal, I reflect on many opportunities and the people that helped me realize and take advantage of them.

I am thankful that I was able to begin my career in a school with great teachers and a great principal, all of whom helped shape who I am today as a principal. Their modeling of how to deal with many academically at-risk, mentally and physically handicapped students provided me with experience and a vision that helps me work with a similar population of students at my school. The master teachers at West School taught me a lot about the art of teaching and how to meet the needs of individual students. My principal taught me how to deal with discipline and plan ahead in the classroom.

I am glad I earned my master's degree at Ashland University. Through their program of study, I completed an administrative internship with Paul Young and learned many hands-on skills that prepared me for my current position. I now benefit from hours of hard work and preparation and use what I learned as a principal. I truly understand the importance of working hard and taking advantage of each opportunity that is given to me.

I am thankful for the many people who have guided and supported me as a teacher, aspiring principal, and now as a principal. A network of influential people has helped me achieve goals that a decade ago I would never have imagined possible. My family has always been and continues to be a great source of support. They understand my busy schedule and have supported me through many long nights and busy weekend activities. I am also thankful for the support I have received from my professional colleagues in the Lancaster City Schools, as well as throughout Ohio and the nation.

Most of all, I am thankful for my mentor. He has devoted much of his time to me and continues to be there, making sure I succeed as a principal. His guidance and understanding allowed me to realize my potential and build upon my strengths and correct my weaknesses. As I grow and gain experience, I continue to seek guidance from my mentor. The relationship of mentor and protégé has been an incredibly valuable learning experience. Although I will begin to depend on my mentor less and less, I will always depend on him as a friend and colleague.

Jeromey M. Sheets
Lancaster, Ohio

Principal mentoring is a human, personal, and shared experience. It requires time and interest, but when the partnership between mentor and mentee becomes strong and meaningful, the rewards are well worth it.

The National Association of Elementary School Principals has developed the PALS (Principals' Advisory Leadership Service) Corps to train and certify principal mentors throughout the United States. The board of directors and staff of the association are to be commended for their foresight and leadership in program and service development. The benefits will be far reaching: membership, increased volunteerism, improved personal performance, support, collaboration, contribution to the field and research, succession planning, people development, and learning. A new generation of principals will enjoy lasting benefits of the sage advice, support, guidance, and friendship of a trained, professional mentor who has "talked the talk and walked the walk." Leadership of our nation's schools will be continuously supported and transferred into capable hands.

Paul G. Young
Lancaster, Ohio

Nothing effective happens in an elementary or middle level school without the endorsement and support of the principal.

—Paul G. Young

The greatest danger for most of us is not that our aim is too high and we will miss it, but that it is too low and we will reach it.

—Michelangelo

Resources

Alvy, H. B., & Robbins, P. (1998). *If I only knew . . . Success strategies for navigating the principalship.* Thousand Oaks, CA: Corwin Press.

Bell, C. R. (2002). *Managers as mentors: Building partnerships for learning.* San Francisco: Berrett-Koehler.

Bennis, W., & Thomas, R. (2002). *Geeks and geezers.* Boston: Harvard Business School Press.

Blanchard, K. (2002). *Whale done! The power of positive relationships.* New York: The Free Press.

Blanchard, K., & Bowles, S. (1993). *Raving fans.* New York: William Morrow.

Blaydes, J. (2003). *The educator's book of quotes.* Thousand Oaks, CA: Corwin Press.

Brock, B., & Grady, M. (2004). *Launching your first principalship: A guide for beginning principals.* Thousand Oaks, CA: Corwin Press.

Brookfield, S. D. (1991). *Understanding and facilitating adult learning: A comprehensive analysis of principles and effective practices.* San Francisco: Jossey-Bass.

Charney, C. (2004). *The portable mentor.* New York: Amacon.

Cottrell, D. (2002). *Monday morning leadership: 8 mentoring sessions you can't afford to miss.* Dallas, TX: Cornerstone Leadership Institute.

Cross, K. P. (1982). *Adults as learners: Increasing participation and facilitating learning.* San Francisco: Jossey-Bass.

Crow, G. M., & Matthews, L. J. (1998). *Finding one's way: How mentoring can lead to dynamic leadership.* Thousand Oaks, CA: Corwin Press.

Daloz, L. A. (1999). *Mentor: Guiding the journey of adult learners.* San Francisco: Jossey-Bass.

Daresh, J. C. (2001). *Beginning the principalship* (2nd ed.). Thousand Oaks, CA: Corwin Press.

Daresh, J. C. (2001). *Leaders helping leaders. A practical guide to administrative mentoring.* Thousand Oaks, CA: Corwin Press.

Daresh, J. C. (2002). *What it means to be a principal.* Thousand Oaks, CA: Corwin Press.

Dunklee, D. (2000). *If you want to lead, not just manage.* Thousand Oaks, CA: Corwin Press.

The Education Alliance at Brown University. (2003). *Making the case for principal mentoring.* Providence, RI: Author.

Fulton, R. (1995). *Common sense leadership.* Berkeley, CA: Ten Speed Press.

Gladwell, M. (2000). *The tipping point: How little things can make a big difference.* Boston: Little, Brown.

Goleman, D. (2002). *Primal leadership: Realizing the power of emotional intelligence.* Boston: Harvard Business School Press.

Grant, J. (2002). *Struggling learners: Below grade or wrong grade.* Rosemont, NJ: Modern Learning Press.

Hoyle, J. R. (2002). *Leadership and the force of love.* Thousand Oaks, CA: Corwin Press.

Johnson, S. (1998). *Who moved my cheese?* New York: G. P. Putnam's Sons.

Johnson, W. B., & Ridley, C. R. (2004). *The elements of mentoring.* New York: Palgrave Macmillan.

Kaser, J., Mundry, S., Stiles, K., & Loucks-Horsley, S. (2002). *Leading every day.* Thousand Oaks, CA: Corwin Press.

Katzenbach, J. R. (2003). *Why pride matters more than money.* New York: Crown Business.

Knowles, M. S. (1980). *The modern practice of adult education: From pedagogy to andragogy.* River Grove, IL: Follett.

Knowles, M. S. (1998). *The definitive classic in adult education and human resource development* (5th ed.). Houston, TX: Gulf Publishing.

Kosmoski, G., & Pollack, D. (2000). *Managing difficult, frustrating, and hostile conversations.* Thousand Oaks, CA: Corwin Press.

Kotter, J. P. (1999). *On what leaders really do.* Boston: The Harvard Business School Press.

Lambert, L. (1998). *Building leadership capacity in schools.* Alexandria, VA: Association for Supervision and Curriculum Development.

Levine, S. R. (2004). *The six fundamentals of success.* New York: Doubleday.

Lieb, S. (1991, Fall). Principles of adult learning. *Vision.* Retrieved July 21, 2004, from http://honolulu.hawaii.edu/intranet/committees/FacDevCom/guidebk/teachtip/adults-2.htm

Littauer, F. (1999). *How to get along with difficult people.* Eugene, OR: Harvest House Publishers.

Lovely, S. (2004). *Staffing the principalship: Finding, coaching, and mentoring school leaders.* Alexandria, VA: Association for Supervision and Curriculum Development.

Maxwell, J. (1995). *Developing the leaders around you.* Nashville, TN: Injoy.

Maxwell, J. (1995). *Leadership 101.* Nashville, TN: Thomas Nelson.

McEwan, E. K. (2003). *10 traits of highly effective principals.* Thousand Oaks, CA: Corwin Press.

Merriam, S. B., & Caffarella, R. S. (1998). *Learning in adulthood: A comprehensive guide* (2nd ed.). San Francisco: Jossey-Bass.

National Academy of Science. (1997). *Advisor, teacher, role model, friend.* Washington, DC: Author.

National Association of Elementary School Principals. (2002). *Leading learning communities: Standards for what principals should know and be able to do.* Alexandria, VA: Author.

Nigro, N. (2003). *The everything coaching and mentoring book*. Avon, MA: Adams Media.

Parker, D. (2003). *Confident communication*. Thousand Oaks, CA: Corwin Press.

Payne, R. (2001). *A framework for understanding poverty*. Highlands, TX: aha! Process.

Portner, H. (2002). *Being mentored: A guide for protégés*. Thousand Oaks, CA: Corwin Press.

Price, A. (2004). *Ready to lead? A story for leaders and their mentors*. San Francisco: Jossey-Bass.

Quaglia, R., & Quay, S. (2003). *Changing lives through the principalship*. Alexandria, VA: National Association of Elementary School Principals.

Ramsey, R. (1999). *Lead, follow, or get out of the way*. Thousand Oaks, CA: Corwin Press.

Ramsey, R. (2003). *School leadership from A to Z. Practical lessons from successful schools and businesses*. Thousand Oaks, CA: Corwin Press.

Schumaker, D., & Sommers, W. (2001). *Being a successful principal*. Thousand Oaks, CA: Corwin Press.

Shea, G. F. (2002). *Mentoring* (3rd ed.). Menlo Park, CA: Crisp Learning.

Tomlinson, C. A., & Allan, S. D. (2000). *Leadership for differentiating schools and classrooms*. Alexandria, VA: Association for Supervision and Curriculum Development.

Whitaker, T. (1999). *Dealing with difficult teachers*. Larchmont, NY: Eye on Education.

Wilmore, E. L. (2002). *Principal leadership: Applying the new Educational Leadership Constituent Council (ELCC) standards*. Thousand Oaks, CA: Corwin Press.

Wilmore, E. L. (2004). *Principal induction: A standards-based model for administrator development*. Thousand Oaks, CA: Corwin Press.

Young, P. (2002, Nov/Dec). Can you hear that sound? *Principal, 82*(2), 68.

Young, P. (2002, Sept/Oct). Monkeys in our schools. *Today's School, 3*(2), 34–36.

Young, P. G. (2004). *You have to go to school, you're the principal! 101 ways to make it better for your students, your staff and yourself*. Thousand Oaks, CA: Corwin Press.

Young, P., & Sheets, J. (2003). *Mastering the art of mentoring principals*. Arlington, VA: KGE Press.

Young, P., Sheets, J., & Kesner, R. (2003, May/June). Mentoring new principals: Two perspectives. *Principal, 82*(5), 48–51.

Zachary, L. J. (2000). *The mentor's guide*. San Francisco: Jossey-Bass.

Zemke, R., & Zemke, S. (1984). 30 things we know for sure about adult learning. *Innovation Abstracts, 6*(8). Retrieved July 21, 2004, from http://honolulu. hawaii.edu/intranet/committees/FacDevCom/guidebk/teachtip/adults-3.htm

Index

**CORWIN
PRESS**

The Corwin Press logo—a raven striding across an open book—represents the union of courage and learning. Corwin Press is committed to improving education for all learners by publishing books and other professional development resources for those serving the field of K–12 education. By providing practical, hands-on materials, Corwin Press continues to carry out the promise of its motto: **"Helping Educators Do Their Work Better."**

NAESP

NATIONAL ASSOCIATION OF ELEMENTARY SCHOOL PRINCIPALS

Serving All Elementary and Middle Level Principals

The 29,500 members of the National Association of Elementary School Principals provide administrative and instructional leadership for public and private elementary and middle schools throughout the United States, Canada, and overseas. Founded in 1921, NAES is today a vigorously independent professional association with its own headquarters building in Alexandria, Virginia, just across the Potomac River from the nation's capital. From this special vantage point, NAESP conveys the unique perspective of the elementary and middle school principal to the highest policy councils of our national government. Through national and regional meetings, award-winning publications, and joint efforts with its 50 state affiliates, NAESP is a strong advocate both for its members and for the 33 million American children enrolled in preschool, kindergarten, and grades 1 through 8.